IMAGES
of America

DENVILLE'S
UNION HILL

Seen here is a Christmas greeting to local soldiers overseas from the Union Hill Civic Association c. 1944.

IMAGES
of America

DENVILLE'S
UNION HILL

Vito Bianco for the
Denville Historical Society & Museum

ARCADIA
PUBLISHING

Published by Arcadia Publishing
Charleston, South Carolina

Library of Congress Catalog Card Number: 2003111119

For all general information, contact Arcadia Publishing:
Telephone 843-853-2070
Fax 843-853-0044
E-mail sales@arcadiapublishing.com
For customer service and orders:
Toll-free 1-888-313-2665

Visit us on the Internet at www.arcadiapublishing.com

This is believed to be the southern approach to the original wooden Openaki Bridge, on Openaki Road, c. 1895.

CONTENTS

ACKNOWLEDGMENTS

J.P. Crayon was a Civil War veteran, teacher, farmer, photographer, genealogist, author, and most notably, local historian. He lived in Union Hill and documented its history just before and after the turn of the 20th century, when many of the sons and daughters of the first settlers were still around to give testimony to the earliest recollections of the area's past. This book would not have been possible without his phenomenal research, transcripts, and records.

The extensive research of former historical society president Rev. Jim D'Angelo on the Den Brook forge sites and former society trustee Cynthia Hinson's detailed research for the Ayres-Knuth Farm historic site application figure prominently in this work, and I am indebted to them. I also relied on the works of Mildred L. Gill and Charles M. toeLear, who wrote the first two exhaustive histories of Denville (in 1955 and 1963, respectively), as well as toeLear's revision in 1988. The 1948 *History of Union Hill*, by Hi-Aimers of the girls 4-H club, proved helpful as well.

Most of the photographs used in this work are part of the Denville Museum's extensive photographic collection. Of particular note is the Cobb Collection, with most photographs taken by Nelson and Leonard Cobb and some by J.P. Crayon. Also used in this work are the photographs in the Illig-Vialard Collection, compiled over many years by Robert Illig and Martha Vialard. I am grateful to a Knuth family member who provided the Knuth family photographs (pages 47 to 51). Longtime Union Hill resident Carolyn Headley provided the photographs of the Union Hill Field Day (pages 96, 98, and 112 to 117). Bill Vandertulip took the photographs on pages 92 to 95 and page 120. Please note the names of individual contributors of single images where they appear in the book; to these lenders I am also grateful. Finally, I want to thank Jillian Bianco and the many people I spoke with along the way for their help in identifying some of the photographs. Special acknowledgement must also go to Daniel Bianco for assisting with proofreading.

Members of the Union Hill Gun Club pose *c.* 1895.

INTRODUCTION

If a stranger passing through town today asked for directions to Pigeon Hill, Franklin, Ninkey, Colerain Forge, or Losey's Brook, most Denville residents would probably think that the stranger was in the wrong place. And yet all of these places were once commonly known in Denville, and they could be found in the part of town we now know as Union Hill.

Three centuries ago, this area was a vast wilderness inhabited only by native people. Then came the settlers, farmers, and forgers alike, who established small communities and claimed the land as their own. Francis Casterline, Obadiah Lum, Jacob Ford Sr., John Losey, John Burwell, Jacob Garrigus, William Winds, Joseph Meeker, William Smith, Jacob Palmer, and Nathaniel Carter were among the earliest pioneers. They endured severe winters and famine, the threat of attack, and violent revolution. Perseverance enabled them to overcome all obstacles, and history will ensure that their deeds will not go unnoticed and their names will not be forgotten.

The Denville Historical Society & Museum is currently overseeing the restoration of an unimposing one-room schoolhouse dating from 1861 and commonly known as the second Union School. Historical society trustee Art Harris chairs Mayor Gene Feyl's Schoolhouse Restoration Committee. No other place in southern Denville so aptly embodies the struggles, hopes, unity, and legacy of Union Hill's early settlers as does this simple schoolhouse. Similarly, the historic Ayres-Knuth Farm remains as testament to the continuity between Union Hill's past and its present. There too, volunteer restoration efforts are ongoing under the cooperative supervision of the mayor's Ayres-Knuth Farm Committee, chaired by Hank Muller.

These restoration projects are most worthy of the community's support. Accordingly, the Denville Historical Society & Museum is dedicating all royalties from the sales of *Denville's Union Hill* to its historic sites restoration fund. As you read this book, do so knowing that in some small but significant way, you are helping to preserve a little piece of Union Hill's fascinating history.

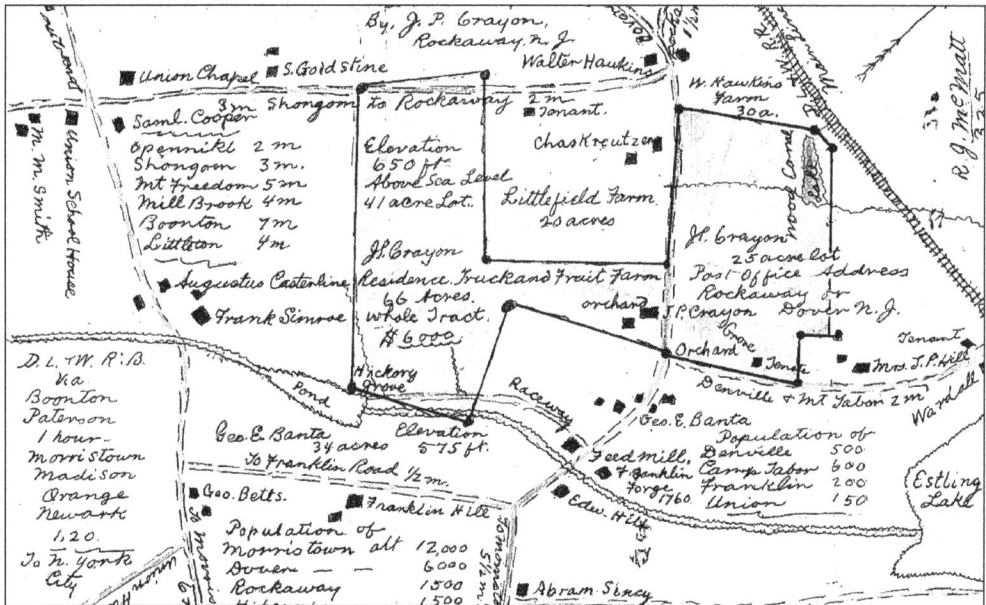

This hand-drawn map of Union Hill was done by J.P. Crayon on March 30, 1903.

A 1656 map by A. Vanderdonck shows the area of New Netherlands that was later known as New Jersey. Also shown are the various native tribes that existed at the time. The map was reprinted in *East Jersey under the Proprietary Governments* (1846).

One

PIGEON HILL

The Lenape, or Delaware, tribe called the land we know as New Jersey Scheyechbi (Shaik-bee), meaning "the land between the water" or "the land of sassafras." The Lenape were a peaceful people who lived throughout Union Hill. Their name signified the original people, since they claimed to be descended from the most ancient of all native ancestry. The Lenape remained in the Morris County area until *c.* 1750. The local legend of Rock Etam recounts the story of how a Lenape princess and two captive settlers escaped her village on foot and disappeared in a snow-covered cave to evade the pursuing tribesmen. The search party reported back to the chief that the rock ate them. Until this day, the hill and cave of legend are known as Rock Etam. The Minisink Trail was a major Lenape thoroughfare that led from the ocean at Manasquan across the Delaware River near Milford and well into Pennsylvania. The trail is believed to have passed through Union Hill roughly following the current course of Route 10 and Mount Pleasant Turnpike. English land speculator Daniel Denton of Long Island likely traveled the Minisink Trail during his exploration of the interior regions of New Jersey *c.* 1665.

All of southern Denville was originally known as Pigeon Hill. For five days in February 1717, one of the worst snowstorms ever recorded hit Morris County. According to some authorities, the snow was said to be 12 feet deep. Many heads of cattle died, and starvation for area residents seemed certain. Local folklore recalls that in the early spring an immense number of wild pigeons mysteriously (or miraculously) appeared, providing the residents with a source of food during that time of great famine. Some believed that the pigeons were sent by "a kind of Providence" to save them from certain starvation. From this event, the name of Pigeon Hill was given to the area. J.P. Crayon, however, provides a different version of the story. He claimed that "it was not out of the order of the day, at that time [that] many of the broad acres of the Smith farm were literally covered with pigeons, hence the name Pigeon Hill, it was a paradise to the early settlers."

Proprietor William Penn (1644–1718) became the first landowner in Pigeon Hill when he exercised his proprietary right to locate lands for himself in the vicinity of Denville in 1715. Two of his lots totaled 3,750 acres and covered much of today's southern Denville and part of neighboring Randolph. Lot No. 74 included the sites of two forges in the area of Pigeon Hill that would later be known as Franklin. Lot No. 77 included the forge sites at Ninkey, Colerain, and Shongum, as well as the sites of the Union Schoolhouse and the Union Chapel.

London merchant and Penn's fellow proprietor John Bellars was known as "the great Quaker philanthropist and social reformer." He never came to America. However, he exercised his proprietary land rights in East New Jersey through his land agent, Thomas Budd. In 1716, John Bellars located for himself a 1,250-acre tract of land adjoining Penn's two lots in Pigeon Hill. Together, the three lots encompassed the entire area of today's Union Hill. The Bellars lot included such contemporary sites as the Ayres-Knuth Farm and Lakeview School. Part of the current boundary between Denville and Parsippany coincides with the ridge that once formed the southeasterly line of the Bellars lot.

With their sizeable land holdings, the Quaker proprietors provided a place of sanctuary and refuge for fellow Quakers. The Pigeon Hill wilderness was considered "a new Promised Land" where Quakers could purchase lots from the proprietors, relocate to, settle, and practice their religion without fear of persecution. Tradition has it that the Underground Railroad, operated with the help of area Quakers, ran through Pigeon Hill and adjoining sections of Randolph.

Jacob Garrigues (1716–1798), who later changed the spelling of his name to Garrigus (see page 18), was a farmer who came to Morris County c. 1748 and settled in the ancestral home known as Peck farm near Littleton and Pigeon Hill. He was born into a prominent Quaker family from Philadelphia that descended from French nobility. However, despite their noble status, because of their Protestant beliefs Garrigus's family was forced to flee to Holland, then to the West Indies, and finally to Philadelphia about the time of Jacob's birth. It was there that they adopted the Quaker faith. Jacob Garrigus's original house still stands in ruins near the Craftsman Farm historic site in Parsippany, just over the border from Denville. His son David was likely born at the Peck farm in 1748. David would own many hundreds of acres of land in Pigeon Hill, including the farm where he resided from 1793 to 1806, next to the Franklin Forge.

Long Islanders also came to the area, perhaps intrigued by the 17th-century explorations of fellow Long Islander Daniel Denton. William Winds (1727–1789) originated from Southold, Long Island, and came to Pigeon Hill as a young man. He established a farm at the intersection of Franklin and Cooper Roads. Winds's forceful personality and robust voice, as it has been described, made him a natural leader. He was instrumental in the establishment of a separate church at Rockaway in 1758. Winds distinguished himself in the French and Indian War of the 1750s and again in the American Revolution, earning the rank of colonel and then general. His most noted accomplishment was the arrest of New Jersey's last royal governor, William Franklin, in 1776. Long Islander Jacob Palmer was a forger who settled along the Den Brook in 1760.

According to tradition, Francis Casterline settled in Pigeon Hill c. 1690. His son Francis died in 1796 at the age of 106. During his life, Francis Jr. had 3 wives and 26 children. His son Joseph (1736–1832) was born in Pigeon Hill. He built the original portion of the house on the corner of Mount Pleasant Turnpike and Franklin Road c. 1782. William "Bold" Smith came to Pigeon Hill from Vermont c. 1750. He married a local Dutch woman named Christiana Derling. At one time, nearly all of the lands between Shongum and Franklin were owned by William Smith and his sons. One source indicates that William Smith built a log home c. 1750, subsequently occupied by his son Garrett (1762–1842), then by his grandson John (1812–1864), and then by his great-grandson Cornelius (born in 1857). Another source claims Peter Smith built the house later in the 18th century (page 83). Peter was the son of Joseph Smith and the grandson of William Smith. A cave known as Peter's Pigpen was located on the mountainside off Smith Road. Peter Smith used this cave to hide pigs from hostile native tribes who ransacked area farms during the 18th century. Local farmers again hid livestock in this cave during the Battle of Springfield in 1780, fearing that the British would invade Morris County.

Peter Hill (1721–1781) came from Germany and settled in Vermont before moving his family to a farm one mile north of Morris Plains in 1768. The Hill family later settled along Cooper and Hill Roads. Obadiah Lum (1708–1783) may have settled at Pigeon Hill as early as 1730, where he is said to have built a home and the first sawmill, as well as the Franklin and Colerain Forges, all before 1740. His son Obadiah was allegedly born at Franklin in 1735. Lum's 1779 will recites that the farm where he lived was on the south side of the Den Brook; however, the precise location has never been determined.

The communities of Franklin and Ninkey emerged in southern Denville in the 18th century, and both were centered around forges of the same names. Union Hill did not develop a separate identity or lend its name to all of southern Denville until after the establishment of the Union School in 1816. Union Hill remained a part of Hanover Township until 1844, then a part of Rockaway Township from 1844 to Denville's separation in 1913.

Eskil Danielson Jr. views the Union Hill landscape from the hill known as Rock Etam. Local Lenapes (and later early setters) used Rock Etam as a lookout to protect against attack from hostile tribes. During the Revolution, it served to warn the population in the event of a possible British invasion. The watch would blow a ram's horn several times to sound the alarm. It was here, according to Lenape legend, where three fugitives vanished in a hilltop cave.

The Lenape often bent saplings into this shape to mark their trails. This tree was found near Lake Openaki in 1913.

William Penn (1644–1718) is shown in old age in this image, based on the postmortem ivory bust by Sylvanus Bevan. Penn was Denville's first recorded landowner, and his 1715 survey is the first map of the Union Hill area. This land would go to his sons, Thomas and Richard, after his death. (Courtesy *The Penns of Pennsylvania and England,* by Arthur Pound.)

Thomas Penn (*c.* 1701–1775), seen here, and his brother Richard Penn (*c.* 1705–1771) inherited much of their father's American holdings. Thomas was the businessman of the family. Rivaling his loyalty to the British Crown was his intense dislike of contemporary Benjamin Franklin. After their meeting in 1758, Franklin wrote, "I conceive . . . a more cordial and thorough contempt for him than I ever felt for any man living." Penn's disdain for Franklin was equally clear: "He is a dangerous man and I should be glad if he inhabited any other country." In 1755, Thomas and Richard Penn began selling off their Union Hill lands. (Courtesy *The Penns of Pennsylvania and England,* by Arthur Pound.)

Lenape tribesmen and colonists engage in trade *c.* 1702. (Courtesy *The Lenape, Archaeology, History, and Ethnography*, by Herbert C. Kraft, the New Jersey Historical Society.)

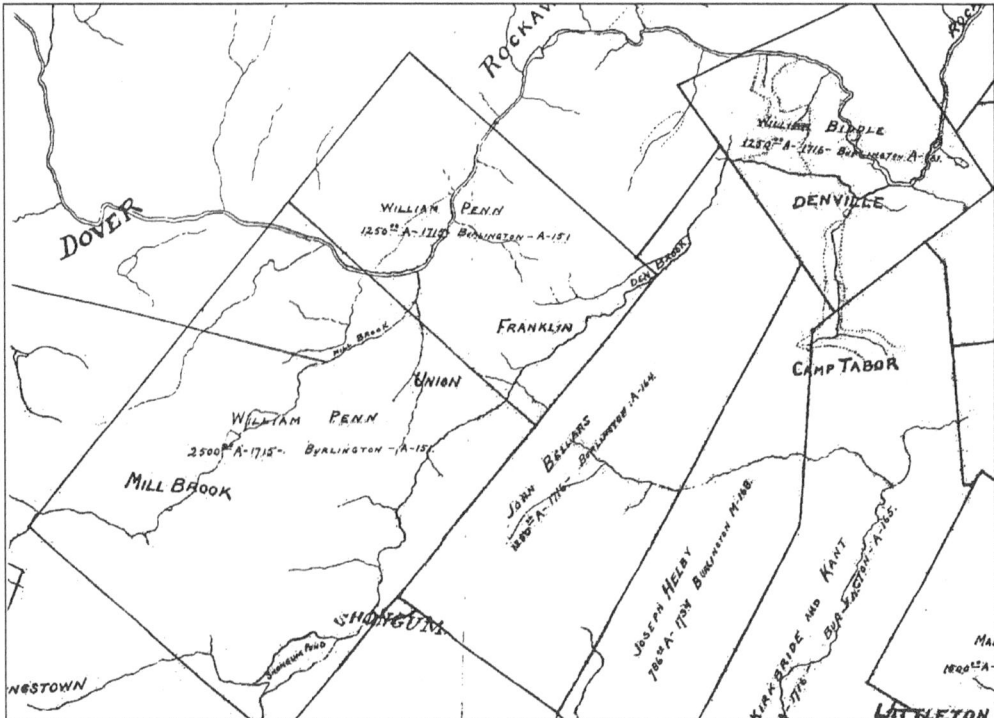

Inaccuracies in the proprietors' surveys led to land disputes, necessitating the replotting of the original claims in 1884. Shown here are William Penn's Lot Nos. 74 and 77, and the Bellars lot. Penn's 1715 survey shows the Den Brook as only a branch of the Rockaway River. It was once known as Losey's Brook, named after John Losey (see chapter 4), who purchased 500 acres along the brook from Penn's sons in 1757.

The c. 1760 Jacob Palmer house stood near the bridge on the western side of Cooper Road, north of the Den Brook. It has sometimes been confused with the nearby Winds house (page 23). The flat terrain and large roadside trees of the Winds property, however, distinguish it from the downward slope and treeless roadside of Palmer's property. Jacob Palmer's descendants would come to own many farms in Franklin.

Before 1765, Nathaniel Carter established the distant farm above (shown c. 1880). His son Aaron Carter (1744–1804) fought in the Revolution and later married Elizabeth Davis. Their son Caleb Carter was born here in 1782, after which his family moved to Newark. Caleb's c. 1803 painting of Mount Vernon hangs in the Newark Museum. Franklin Forge owner David Garrigus purchased this farm in 1793; he built a stone house and resided here until in 1806. A man named McComley bought the farm from Garrigus. John Hill bought it in 1809 and established the Hill farm. Trobridge Mountain, or Union Hill (background), rises 1,033 feet.

Seen is an enlargement of the Union Hill area from *Map of a Group of Iron Mines in Morris County*, drawn by G.M. Hopkins under the direction of George H. Cook, the state geologist, in 1867. Shown are the old forge at Franklin, the schoolhouse at Union, the Rock Etam of legend, Ninkey, and the little-known Frenchman's Mine (today in Randolph). There are no claim records for Frenchman's Mine and no extensive mining was done at the site. A field examination of the mine reported small, shallow pits, one of which was cut with scattered crystals of magnetite.

A 1762 letter to Benjamin Franklin reads, "Worthy Sir. . . . You have been pleased once to do a great favour for my Mother with Respect to finding her Father the late Mr. Ralph for which you have laid us all under lasting Obligation to you. . . . I am Worthy Sir with the Greatest Respect your much Obliged and most Obedient servant. Isaac Garrigues."

Isaac Garrigues was born into a prominent Philadelphia Quaker family in 1741. He was the eldest son of Samuel Garrigues and Mary Ralph. Benjamin Franklin was a friend of Isaac's maternal grandfather, poet James Ralph, who accompanied Franklin on a trip to England in 1724. Ralph remained in England, deserting his American family and marrying again. Benjamin Franklin attended the wedding of Isaac's parents in Philadelphia on July 10, 1740. Isaac's uncle Jacob settled near Littleton and Pigeon Hill c. 1748. The connection between Isaac's family and Benjamin Franklin provides one theory as to how the Franklin section of Union Hill got its name.

Two

FRANKLIN

The Franklin, or Franklin Hill, section of Denville has all but vanished from modern maps and memories. The once thriving and distinct village of Franklin that was centered at the point where Cooper Road crosses the Den Brook has today been absorbed into Union Hill. Franklin Road in Denville, Franklin Road in Randolph (which turns into Palmer Road in Denville), and Franklin Avenue in Denville and Rockaway are all that remain of this once vibrant community.

There are many sources that indicate that Franklin was initially the central locale of the Pigeon Hill of lore. The one-time Carter farm that existed in the 18th century (see page 14) was referenced in a 1793 deed as being in Pigeon Hill. The plotting of that farm clearly shows that it was located in what later became known as Franklin, adjacent to the Franklin Forge. An 1870s news article about the Ayres family indicated that they were from Pigeon Hill, although their farm (discussed in chapter 3) was located in the area more commonly identified as Franklin by that time. A hand-drawn map in the collection of the Morristown Library, dating from the early 19th century, shows Pigeon Hill to be centered at the intersection of Cooper Road and Mount Pleasant Turnpike. While Pigeon Hill was an established community by the mid-1700s, the name Franklin would not become more commonly identified with the area until some indeterminable time after the establishment of the Franklin Forge.

The original surveys of proprietors William Penn, in 1715, and John Bellars, in 1716, are the first maps of the Franklin Hill area. Penn's lot No. 74 included the location of the Franklin Forge. The existence of a forge at Franklin Hill has always been known to local residents and local historians, although very little factual information has been written about the forge. Researchers have concluded that there were likely two forges at Franklin—an earlier forge, built between 1735 and 1759, and a later forge, constructed between 1774 and 1777.

Obadiah Lum likely built the first forge along the Den Brook at Franklin in 1759, on the land he purchased from Thomas and Richard Penn that same year. The precise location of the first forge has not been documented. Other research suggests, however, that either Morris County pioneer Col. Jacob Ford (1704–1777) or Lum (with the financial backing of Ford before he actually owned the land) may have built the first forge as early as 1735. Historian J.P. Crayon wrote that Col. Jacob Ford built the first Franklin Forge before 1750. According to Crayon's research, by 1750, the Franklin Forge was referred to as one of the "Colonel's old forges." Crayon's research may be supported by an advertisement that was placed in the *New York Gazette* or the *Weekly Post Boy* on March 10, 1755, by Thomas and Richard Penn, offering to sell their late father's lot No. 74 "on Rockaway, near Col. Ford's Lower Iron Works." However, this reference could also be to the former Job Allen ironworks (c. 1730) near Denville center, purchased by Ford in 1748.

John Cobb, Thomas Brown, and Stephen Jackson built the second forge at the location they purchased from Obadiah Lum in 1774. This more generally known Franklin Forge site is located on the northerly side of Cooper Road, on the western bank of the Den Brook, just over the bridge.

Jacob Garrigues and his sons David, Isaac, Jacob Jr., and John had already abandoned their Quaker faith and joined the Rockaway Presbyterian Church when they joined to fight in the Revolutionary War. This caused a rift with the Quaker branch of the family in Philadelphia, resulting in Jacob's official excommunication from the Quaker faith. Jacob changed the spelling of his surname from Garrigues to Garrigus in order to distinguish his family from the other.

David Garrigus owned and operated the Franklin Forge beginning in 1785. In 1793, he purchased the 117-acre Carter farm adjacent to the forge. He sold the forge to Isaac Canfield in 1806.

Around the time of the Revolutionary War, Franklin Hill was a well-populated community of at least 20 or more families. Jacob Palmer came from Long Island and settled at Franklin c. 1760. He was a forger by trade and likely worked at the Franklin Forge. He married Phebe Lyon in 1768. Their children were born at Franklin beginning in 1769. David Moore was a Revolutionary War soldier who lived about a half-mile northeast of William Winds's house at Franklin (see page 23). He married Rachel Haden, his second wife, in 1777. Her father, William Haden, built the Hoppler house at Franklin in 1767. In more recent memory, this house was the main house of the Poulous farm and still stands at 304 Palmer Road. Eliakim Anderson also built a house in Franklin in 1767. After the Revolution, Nathaniel Dickerson (born in 1758) built and lived in a house about 150 yards north and opposite of Winds's house. John Hall (born in 1760) came from Saybrook, Connecticut, and settled first at Franklin, then Denville center.

By vocation, through investment or because of marriage, most of these families were associated with the Franklin Forge. Often, the principal owners of the forge through the years were officers in the Rockaway Presbyterian Church. In fact, Franklin was one of the settlements of the Rockaway parish. Even though the Rockaway meetinghouse was the center for worship and government in those early days, there can be identified at Franklin Hill a distinct community centered on the forge. Through the next century, it would continue to flourish with a sawmill, gristmill, cider mill, distillery, organ factory, and even a school.

A school at Franklin operated from c. 1777 to 1816. An entry in the handwritten ledger of J.P. Crayon indicates that c. 1810, Joseph J. Ayres (1806–1882), the son of Daniel Ayres (see page 38), "[first] went to school in a frame building located near Captain Allan Lee Bassett's gate at the south corner of the Union cross-roads." Crayon's description places this schoolhouse on the south side of Franklin Road, near the former home of Silas S. Palmer (see page 30), which was later owned by Henry B. Palmer (at the intersection of Franklin Road and Franklin Avenue). Another account sites the schoolhouse closer to the intersection of Palmer Road and Franklin Avenue. The Franklin School predates the Revolution as it was already considered an old schoolhouse when David Cooper (1801–1899) and Joseph Ayres first attended school there in the early 19th century. It was abandoned when the stone schoolhouse was built in the Union School district in 1816 (see chapter 5). Some of the teachers at the Franklin School were Charles Sammis, Daniel Lampson, Sylvanus Hance, Betsy Losey, Charles Jackson, and George Stickle. Abijah Conger taught at the school occasionally when the regular teacher was absent or sick or no teacher was engaged. The children from Franklin went to the Denville school whenever the Franklin School was closed. However, they also attended school in Littleton, Ninkey, Rockaway, and Dover, and students from those localities, in turn, attended school in Franklin when they were without a teacher.

Seen here is downtown Franklin *c.* 1880. This photograph was taken near the intersection of Cooper and Hill Roads, facing west. A Hill residence is in the foreground, and the large building in the center is the gristmill. Crayon claimed that *c.* 1730, Obadiah Lum built a house 300 yards due south of his own house. Jim D'Angelo plotted Crayon's claim and found that "Lum's house [would be] in the field on the south side of the [Den] brook just below the swamp." This location corresponds to Lum's will.

This is a photograph of the original stone bridge over the Den Brook on Cooper Road. This bridge could have been as much as 150 years old at the time the photograph was taken *c.* 1880. The building shown is part of the gristmill. The second Franklin Forge was located near the waterline on the lower right side.

The intersection of Cooper and Franklin Roads is shown *c.* 1900. The view faces north up Franklin Road toward Denville.

This photograph was taken close to the Hill Cemetery on Cooper Road in a cornfield of the Hill farm *c.* 1880. The farm's orchards are just beyond the cornfield. In the distance, facing toward Denville center, is Estling Lake. Snake Hill, one of Denville's four Revolutionary War lookouts, is to the left.

Joseph Percy Crayon (1841–1908) is seen along the walkway to his house c. 1901. As a teacher, he changed his surname from Crain to Crayon, believing that his students would pay more attention to him with the latter as his last name.

A local woman takes a ride down Cooper Road in her horse and buggy in the early 1900s.

William Franklin (1730–1813), New Jersey's last royal governor (1762–1776), remained loyal to England during the Revolution despite attempts by his father, Benjamin Franklin, to sway him to the American cause. Col. William Winds was ordered to watch him closely. This portrait was done by Mather Brown. The following is a note written by Winds to William Franklin: "To His Excellency William Franklin, Esq.—I desire that you will give me your Word and Honour that you will not depart this Province till I know the Will & Pleasure of the Continental Congress concerning the Matter. From Your Humble Servant, William Winds."

A violent knock at the door of the c. 1764 proprietary house in Perth Amboy (above) awoke the governor as armed men surrounded his residence on the morning of January 8, 1776. Colonel Winds's letter was delivered, demanding an immediate answer. Franklin responded, "Sir, I have not the least Intention to quit the Province, nor shall I unless compelled by Violence. Were I to act otherwise it would not be consistent with my Declarations to the Assembly, nor my Regard for the good People of the Province. Your Humble servant, William Franklin."

By order of the Provincial Congress, Col. William Winds arrested Governor Franklin on June 19, 1776. The governor was tried for treason at Princeton and ordered imprisoned in Connecticut before escaping to England. In 1777, Winds was promoted to brigadier general, the highest rank of all the area's Revolutionary War veterans. Perhaps the name Franklin became synonymous with Pigeon Hill to honor the legendary general who resided in this house, located at the intersection of Franklin and Cooper Roads.

Seen is the interior of the Winds house c. 1890. As a justice of the peace in 1765, Winds refused to use stamped paper for legal documents in protest of the Stamp Act. He used the bark from white birch trees instead of the paper. Winds represented Morris County in the New Jersey General Assembly in 1772 and 1775 and as a delegate to the Provincial Congress in New Brunswick in 1776.

Seen here on the left are J.P. Crayon and his first wife, Minnie Ruhama Webb (1838–1886). She was the daughter of Abner Webb and Sarah J. Davenport Webb. The photograph was taken c. 1868. On the right is Crayon's second wife, Susie H. Hill (1855–1912). She was the daughter of John O. Hill and Nancy Talmadge Hill.

On the left, in a c. 1868 photograph, is Mary Strait Crain (1819–1872), the mother of J.P. Crayon. On the right, in a photograph also taken c. 1868, is James Crain (1812–1879), the father of J.P. Crayon.

Seen is J.P. Crayon's grave at Hill Cemetery on Cooper Road. The earliest marked grave dates from 1836; however, the cemetery may contain older unmarked graves. The cemetery's location next to a church has created the misconception for some that it is associated with the church. Actually, the cemetery is all that remains of the once sprawling Hill farm. Scout troops, neighbors, church members, and others volunteer to maintain the cemetery.

This is the Silas Halsey Palmer house, located at 331 Franklin Road. The right side of the house is the original section, built before 1853. The left side is a later addition. This was J.P. Crayon's last residence in Franklin.

This photograph, taken on Cooper Road by Percy Davenport c. 1910, shows the Shawger cider mill (center), formerly an old gristmill, as well as the Cooper Road Bridge over the Den Brook.

Walter T. Shawger (1876–1950) and his wife, Serena May Card Shawger (1874–1940), owned and operated the Shawger cider mill on Cooper Road c. 1905. The mill burned c. 1917–1919, and it was rebuilt by Walter Shawger, who later ran it outside as a one-man operation.

This photograph, taken from the Cooper Road Bridge in 1891, shows the barns and the other outbuildings of the J. Palmer farm along Cooper Road. The corner of the original Jacob Palmer house is barely visible on the left.

This image was taken in October 1891 from a slightly different angle than the one above. The Jacob Palmer house, on the left, is more clearly visible. The woman in the center is likely a member of the Palmer family.

Shown is a summertime view of the intersection of Franklin Road (in the foreground to the right) and Cooper Road (to the left). Local residents and frequent travelers of these roads will recognize this intersection as the place where a round mirror allows those stopped on Franklin Road to see cars coming up the hill on Cooper Road. The barns are part of J.P. Crayon's farm (later Cobb's farm).

The same intersection is shown here but in a slightly closer view. The photograph was taken after a snowstorm on November 29, 1892.

This is a summertime view of the stretch of Franklin Road between Cooper Road and Franklin Avenue, facing west. The house and fence on the left belonged to J.P. Crayon and later the Cobb family. The house in the distance belonged to A. Basset (formerly the Tompkins house).

This is the same view as above, but the photograph was taken after the snowstorm on November 29, 1892. The distant Basset house can be seen more clearly.

This image is believed to be a view along Franklin Road (possibly Basset's home) c. 1895, near the intersection with Franklin Avenue.

Silas Southard Palmer (1804–1876) built the above house at the crossroads of Franklin Road and Franklin Avenue c. 1834. S.S. Palmer owned several houses in Franklin, including the old Winds house (later Crayon's house). The original part of this Palmer house is architecturally consistent with one built in 1834. A 1986–1987 cultural resources survey of Morris County concluded that this house was built c. 1836 with later additions.

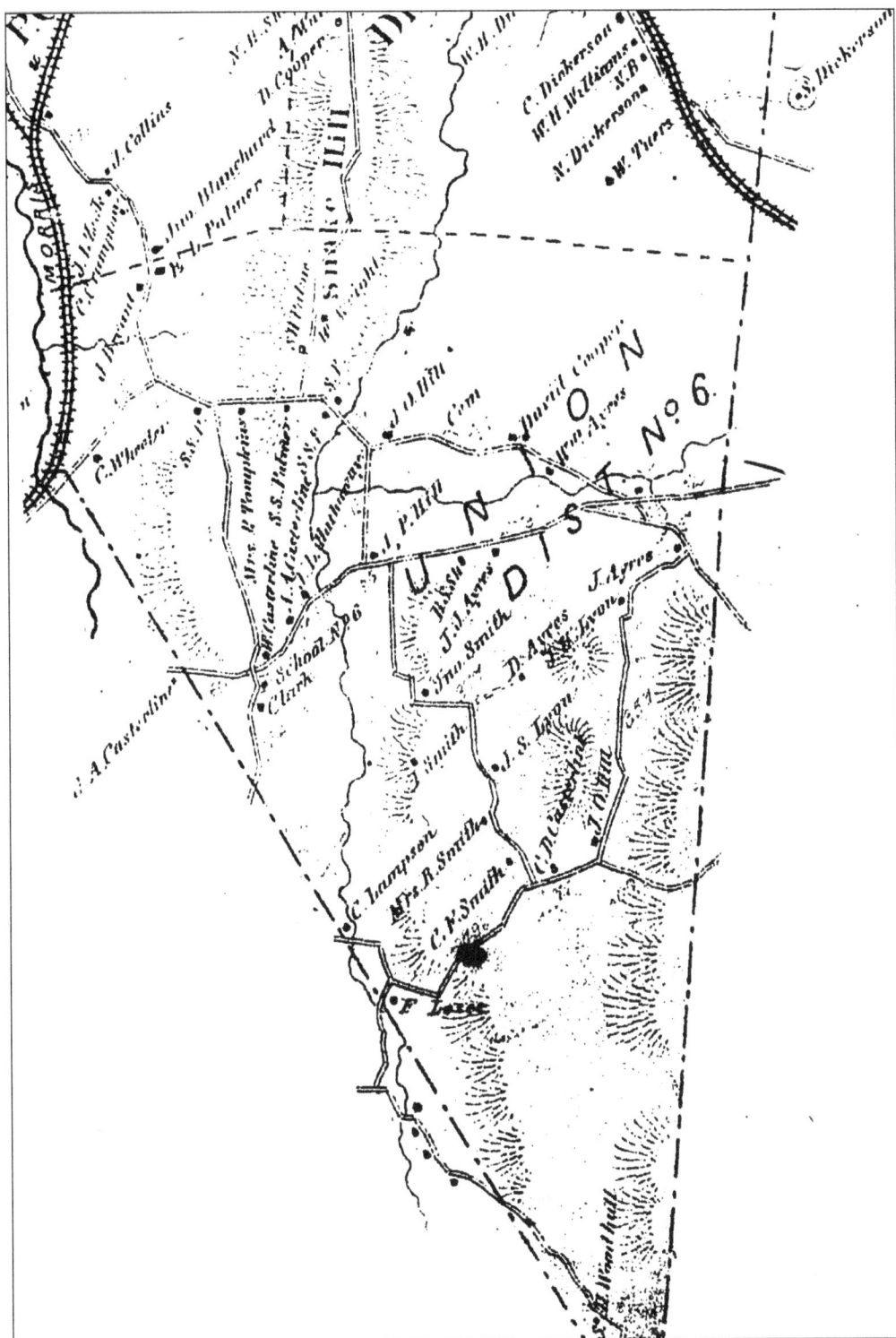

This enlargement of the Union district in the 1868 Beers map of Rockaway Township is the first detailed map of the area and has proved to be a valuable resource for researchers and historians.

William S. Wright (1843–1912) was the owner of the Wright organ factory, located on Cooper Road alongside the Delaware, Lackawanna & Western Railroad tracks (see page 81) across from Wright's house on Franklin Road. The business employed six people who were all specialists in the field.

Mary J. Palmer Wright (1843–1927) was the wife of William Wright. The business of manufacturing organs prospered in the late 19th century, and larger facilities were built. In 1898, the company moved to Dover and converted to an organ tuning and repair business.

The Delaware, Lackawanna & Western Railroad crossed Franklin Road by William and Mary Wright's house. This c. 1893 photograph shows William Wright standing by the railroad gate. The gatekeeper's house is behind him, and the Wright house is in the background.

John Gallagher was the gatekeeper at Wright's railroad crossing. He earned $1 per day.

HISTORY

OF THE

COOPER FAMILY

DAVID COOPER

BY J. P. CRAYON, ROCKAWAY, N. J.

ROCKAWAY, N. J.:
ROCKAWAY PUBLISHING HOUSE.
1894.

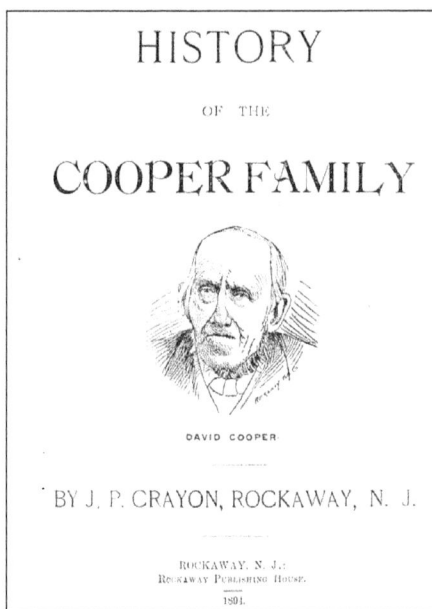

J.P. Crayon authored this pamphlet on the Cooper family in 1894. The illustration is of David Cooper (1801–1899). David was born in a house on Franklin Road built by his father, William Cooper. David married Anna Ayres in 1822. Their first home was near Mount Tabor. They moved, according to Crayon, to the house at Cooper Road and Birch Run Avenue (now the Hardin house) on April 1, 1831.

Seen on the left is Silas Edwin Cooper (1849–1911), the 11th child of David and Anna Cooper. He was born at the Cooper Road home. On the right is Loretta D. Smith, the wife of Silas E. Cooper and the daughter of John J. Smith. They had nine children. The family later moved to Nevada.

This Cooper family reunion was held *c.* 1895 at David Cooper's home. Once, in 1824, David Cooper traveled to Hamilton, Ohio, to meet with the Garrigus family, who had moved there in 1806. At nearly 100 years old, David had 12 children, 36 grandchildren, 48 great-grandchildren, and 4 great-great-grandchildren. David is seated in the center on the porch. Standing in front, second from the left, is William H. Casterline (see chapter 5).

Seen here are five generations of the Cooper family. David Cooper is seated. His daughter Sarah Ann Fichter is standing to the far right. Her son Daniel C. Fichter is standing. His daughter Martha Jane Berryman is seated. Berryman's child is to the far left.

Mary "Polly" Garrigus Ayres (1783–1875), pictured *c.* 1874, belonged to the Rockaway Presbyterian Church since 1822 and married the widowed Daniel Ayres in 1823. Her father, John Garrigus (1760–1850), was the younger brother of David Garrigus, making Polly a first cousin to her husband's first wife, Hannah. Polly Ayres died on Christmas Eve 1875 at age 92.

Three

THE AYRES-KNUTH FARM

Little is known of David Garrigus (1748–1815), but he has been described as "easily excited, losing his balance in many instances." During the Revolutionary War, Garrigus served as a private in Capt. Josiah Hall's company, the Eastern Battalion of Morris County, New Jersey. While Garrigus was doing guard duty for Foster Williams of Shongum, Williams bet with some of the soldiers in the company that he could take Garrigus's musket away from him while Garrigus was at his post. Williams went up to Garrigus demanding his musket. When Garrigus refused, Williams tried to take it by force. Garrigus shot Williams, who died a few hours later.

The success of Garrigus's business and farming enterprises in Franklin allowed him to acquire hundreds of acres of land by 1800. Later that year, his daughter Hannah Garrigus (1783–1821) married Daniel Ayres. On May 10, 1803, David Garrigus sold 105 acres to his son-in-law, who established the now historic farm that would remain in the Ayres family for nearly a century. Soon after, David Garrigus began to sell off the rest of his property in Franklin in preparation for a move to Hamilton, Ohio. The historical record gives no explanation why David Garrigus and several family members moved to Ohio in 1806. In Ohio, Garrigus's oldest son, Jeptha Garrigus (born in 1776), built a gristmill in Hamilton in 1810 later known as Jackson's Mill. Most of the family remained in Ohio, but some members ended up in Michigan and Indiana. David Garrigus is buried in Hamilton, Ohio, with his wife, Abigail Losey (1756–1817), the daughter of James Puff Losey (see page 53).

David Garrigus's son-in-law Daniel Ayres (1778–1856) was born in Woodbridge, New Jersey. His father, Robert Ayres (1738–1787), came from Woodbridge to Franklin (or Rockaway) perhaps as early as 1760 and then returned to Woodbridge after he was married. Daniel's mother, Anna Jackson Ayres (1746–1816) was born at Rockaway and was the daughter of Gen. Joseph Jackson (1710–1769), the patriarch of the prominent Jackson family, who settled at Rockaway *c.* 1731.

In his early life, Daniel Ayres learned the shoemaker's trade, serving a seven-year apprenticeship. This trade provided him with an additional source of income, particularly in the early years of his marriage. Daniel Ayres first appeared on the tax rolls in August 1803. He was shown at that time to own 105 improved acres and two heads of cattle. Anna Sabina Ayers was born to Hannah and Daniel Ayres "at Franklin" on November 14, 1803. In 1822, she married David Cooper (see pages 34 and 35). The Reverend Barnabas King of Rockaway performed the ceremony at the Daniel Ayres house. Anna's daughter Sarah Ann Cooper Fichter (1829–1920) described the marriage custom of the time in an interview she gave to Charles Platt on January 10, 1920. The bride and groom arrived on horseback to be married. A wedding banquet was prepared at the bride's home, typically with roast turkey. If either the bride or groom or both refused to get married, it seems that "the guests made away with the banquet just the same."

In the years following 1803, Hannah and Daniel Ayres would see their family and farm expand. Joseph Jackson Ayers was born in 1806, and he was buried at Hill Cemetery in 1882. David Garrigus Ayres was born in 1807, Abigail Ayres was born in 1810, and Hannah M.

Ayres was born in 1812. Between 1803 and 1822, Daniel Ayres owned as many as two horses and up to seven heads of cattle. Little is known beyond the fact that he, like many of his neighbors, was an active member of the Rockaway Presbyterian Church, where he sang in the choir. Daniel was received in the church in 1808. After the death of his first wife, Hannah, in 1821, Daniel married for a second time in 1823. His new bride was Mary "Polly" Garrigus (1783–1875), a cousin to his late wife. Daniel and Polly Ayres had two children, William in 1824 and John in 1826.

Daniel Ayres's other business dealings included a partnership in the Dover furnace, or ironworks, beginning in 1830. By 1840, teenagers William and John Ayres were working as farm hands with their aging father. In 1850, the Daniel Ayres farm was valued at $2,500, which indicates that his operation had grown beyond mere subsistence farming. This is also evident from the number of resident farm hands, female housekeepers, and caretaker couples that became commonplace at the Ayres farm since the 1830s.

Daniel Ayres had a small dairy farming operation where six milch cows produced an annual yield of 500 pounds of butter, likely churned on-site. Poultry played little or no role on his farm. He raised sheep for profit, but the swine he raised were solely for use by the family. Like so many farmers of the period, Daniel Ayres established a small family orchard, which was located directly behind and to the west of the farmhouse. The excess fruit from the orchard was sold for additional income, along with honey. While the historical record is unclear, it was likely financial reasons, combined with Daniel Ayres's advanced age and declining heath, that precipitated the transfer of the farm to John Ayres and his wife sometime before September 1852, although no deed of transfer to them can be found. However, they would not own the farm for long. William Ayres purchased the 105-acre farm from his brother John on September 7, 1852.

William Ayers (1824–1900) attended school until age 13 and then began to work on the family farm. Intending to relocate out west, he traveled to Minnesota territory in 1848, then to Rock Island, Illinois, where, in 1849, he purchased a farm and mill. He returned home to settle some business and found his parents in poor health. They persuaded him to sell his western interests and remain. By 1850, he was back on the family farm and owned real estate of his own, valued at $250.

On the last day of 1854, William Ayres married Phebe Smith (born in 1831) of Pigeon Hill. She was the daughter of William Smith (1804–1854) and Harriet Fisher Smith (1809–1895). Her great-grandfather was the same William Smith who came to the area from Vermont c. 1750 (see page 10). Phebe's mother, Harriet Fisher Smith, was the eldest child of Charles and Hannah Maria Fisher, who immigrated to America from Germany either just before or just after Harriet's birth. In 1855, William and Phebe Ayres had their first child, a son they named George. Their daughter Emma was born in 1857, and their other daughter, Martha, was born in 1859.

From 1850 to 1855, William was in the business of hauling charcoal to Newark and other neighboring cities. Then, c. 1855, he began selling wood, railroad ties, and timber to the Delaware, Lackawanna & Western Railroad Company and to the Erie Railroad at Paterson. Like his father, William continued raising sheep on the farm. In 1859, he owned 22 sheep that provided 93 pounds of wool for sale.

In the years just prior to the Civil War, the agriculture of the region entered a period of transition. It was at this dawning of change that Daniel Ayers died at the age of 78. His son William immediately assumed the increased responsibilities inherent in farm ownership. Within a decade after Daniel Ayres's death, New Jersey agriculture would undergo significant changes due primarily to competition from large farms in the newly settled western states. For example, western competition led William to reduce the size of his sheep flock to nine by 1869, and by 1880, he raised no sheep at all. William Ayres would be required to make other such changes in his farming methods in order to retain his land and continue a profitable operation. He extended his field of operations to other lines by engaging in general farming and horticultural pursuits.

The carriage house pictured here was built c. 1850. Besides its obvious use, it was also used as a distillery and a forge.

This is a painted tray depicting the farmhouse at the Ayres-Knuth Farm as it appeared in the 19th century. The left section of the house no longer exists. It could have been the original 1803 farmhouse that was later removed from the newer section of the house that dates from the 1850s. The Ayres family owned this farm from 1803 to 1896. The Knuth family owned it from 1906 to 1996. The farm is on the New Jersey and National Registers of Historic Places. (Courtesy an Ayres descendant.)

William Ayres employed full-time hired hands and a housekeeper by the late 19th century, paying annual wages (including board) of $625, when the average farmer paid just $214. John Garrigus (1826–1886), a farm hand and William's first cousin, is likely the man standing by the wagon in this c. 1880 view. Other farm hands were Frank Dutch, Charles Friday, Edward Mandigo, Frank McPeet, and Paul Vetter. Elamanda Rockwell was a female housekeeper during this period.

William and Phebe Ayres's holdings grew significantly during the 1850s, with land and personal property valued at $5,000. The main portion of the farmhouse (above left, c. 1868) was built during this period of prosperity. The smaller section (right) is likely older and may even be the original farmhouse. William Ayres's house was uncluttered by excessive ornamentation and was austere by urban standards. It is evident that Ayres desired comfortable, modern surroundings for his family but was not inclined toward ostentation. As a successful farmer, Ayres realized that maintaining the land was his priority, and excess cash was earmarked for the purchase of additional acreage or equipment or for the construction and repair of necessary outbuildings. The Ayres family continued to grow in the 1860s with the births of a daughter, Mary, in 1861; a son, Lawrence, in 1863; and another son, Frank, in 1867. Daughters Amanda and Hattie were born in 1868 and 1869, respectively. By 1870, the Ayres farm was still thriving and valued at $8,000 (land and personal property). The man standing with the child is likely William Ayres with his son Lawrence.

Dover, N. J., March 28, 1885

Mr. Lawrence Ayres

BOUGHT OF **WM. AYRES,**

—FARMER AND DEALER IN—

·:· Farm Produce, Cider and Cider Vinegar. ·:·

Cord Wood and Wood Sawed in Stove Lengths.

1884						
Mch	12	Cash	1		$134	38
	13	do	1			
	22	To Cart stone	1	50		
April	9	Brick & Lime	3	20		
	12	Cash Zindle	5	—		
	15	self 1.00 Zindle 1.00	2	—		
	19	Zindle	10	—		
		Lime	2	60		
		Lumber	15	47		
		Apple trees			16	00
		Lumber & stone Palmer	8	30		
May	13	Cash	1	—		
	26=27	Cash	11	90		
June	21	Cash	1	—		
July	4	Cash	10	—		
Nov	21	Cash	14	—		
Dec	1st	By 8 mos			108	—
		Error in Lumber				65
	20	Pay Tax Hanover	83			
	24	Cash Overcoat	13	—		
	28	cash	12	—	12	
Feby	16	Apples Rodner	2	88		
	18	Check Rodner	10	90	12	
		Hay	35			
		Cash Hamilton Cash Newark	2	—	12	
Mch	2=7=9	Cash	13		12	—
			$178.55		$307.01	

There has been much dispute among historians concerning the Ayres distillery. Munsell's history indicates that George Ayres (1855–1893) built the distillery in 1868. This seems improbable, however, since George was just 13 in 1868. Mildred Gill wrote that c. 1840, "William Ayres and his son George operated a cider mill and distillery at what is now known as Knuth's Pond on Cooper Road." In 1840, however, William Ayres was only 16 and George had not yet been born. J.P. Crayon claimed that Abijah Conger built the Cooper Road (cider) mill in 1820 that was later operated by the Ayres family. However, Jim D'Angelo found no conclusive evidence of an earlier distillery. Harry B. Weiss wrote that Conger's distillery was built on the north side of the "road leading from Dover to Franklin." If this is Cooper Road, the Conger site cannot be the Ayres distillery since the Ayres property was on the south side of the road. The Ayres farm ledger above shows that cider and cider vinegar were sold at the farm in 1885.

William Ayres most likely built what is known locally as the "Billy Ayres Distillery" c. 1868. He likely operated the early distillery as well, but by 1880, George Ayres was a distiller by profession, running the distillery on his father's farm, one of just two operating in the township at that time. George Ayres and his wife, Lillian (born in 1860), had a son, Aldean, in 1877. Tragically, in 1893, George Ayers died at the young age of 37. The following year, Aldean Ayres married a woman named Anna, and the young couple lived on the farm with William and Phebe Ayres. It seems that the Ayres distillery that operated for about 25 years died with George Ayres. There is no indication that William Ayres continued the distillery operation, neither does it appear that Aldean picked up where his father left off. The stone foundations of the distillery (above) are all that remain of the once thriving operation, along with the ruins of the earthen dam that provided the power necessary to grind and press the fruit.

As increasing notions of family privacy grew after the Civil War, farm hands were more frequently boarded in separate buildings, rather than with the farmer and his family. The Ayres tenant house (above), built c. 1875, satisfied this need for privacy, while its location near the main house ensured that William Ayres could maintain a sharp eye on his laborers. Many of resident farm hands were German, Austrian, or Irish immigrants.

Unlike many local farmers, William Ayres never concentrated solely on poultry or dairy farming but also sold grains, hay, wood, and railroad ties. He increased the size of his farm and, at one time, owned over 500 acres. He improved his property with several outbuildings (above), most of which are still standing. By 1880, despite the depression of 1873–1879, William's farm was valued at $17,400, a 500 percent increase over 30 years.

William Ayres changed his farming operation with the times. He moved away from raising sheep and slowly increased the size of his dairy herd. The number of milch cows he owned in 1859 (six) doubled by 1880. He also pursued poultry farming on a modest scale. By 1880, he owned 200 chickens and reported the sale of 1,500 eggs. One of the farm's two late-19th-century chicken coops is the distance above.

By 1880, William Ayres stopped planting wheat and cut production of corn and buckwheat to half of what it was in 1860. Oats production remained unchanged but was used primarily for feed, as livestock herds, particularly horses, increased. In 1859, William Ayres sold $30 worth of orchard produce. By 1879, some 400 fruit trees were planted on 16 acres devoted to apple, peach, pear, and other fruit cultivation, generating $200 from orchard products.

45

Lawrence Ayres fended off creditors in 1890 by purchasing the farm at sheriff's sale. This allowed his parents to remain there until William's retirement in 1896, during difficult times. William and Phebe's son George died in 1893, and their daughter Amanda followed in 1896. Lawrence sold the farm to Albert Kent on May 26, 1896, ending the Ayres family's 93-year tenure. William Ayres died in 1900 at the new home he built for Phebe.

The smokehouse, seen here c. 1828, is the farm's oldest surviving structure. Before conveying the farm again, Albert Kent granted certain rights to William Ayres that may have included the orchard rights, and a tenancy for Aldean Ayers to remain on the farm. Perhaps the last Ayres born on the farm was Aldean's daughter Lillian in 1897, when census records show her family was living in Franklin on a farm they did not own.

Martin Knuth (1860–1935) and Anna Knuth (1861–1950), seen *c.* 1934 with their sons, were born in Germany and, in 1881, were married there. They came to America aboard the *Lessing*, arriving on June 29, 1882. Immigration mistakenly listed them as Anna and Martin Knutle (a butcher) from Prussia. Census takers made similar errors; Martin Knuth was once listed as Martin Kanute. Their first child, John Knuth (seen behind Anna), was born in April 1884.

Living in Randolph by 1886, they purchased their first farm (42 acres) from John O. Hill, near the top of Zeek Road, containing a house and several outbuildings. Despite its high elevation and rocky terrain, the farm proved successful and was mortgage free by 1900. Born at this farm were, seen here from left to right, Martin Jr. (a twin to Andrew, born in 1899), Hedwig "Hattie" (1893–1947), Frank (1902–1990), Andrew (a twin to Martin, born in 1899), Anna (born in 1890), and Susie (1896–1990). Jacob Knuth (second from the right) was born on the new farm in 1906.

Reduced to 65 acres since 1896, the Knuths bought the old Ayres farm on June 4, 1906, and would prosper there until a fire claimed the barn in 1936 (see page 50). The farm continued to expand until 1920. In 1907 alone, more than 148 acres were purchased, and by 1915, there was no mortgage. The farmhouse interior (above) was left unchanged. There was only limited electricity by 1965 and no indoor plumbing. The outhouse was used until 1990.

Anna's granddaughter Marie (center) and the Knuth women are seen c. 1936. The Knuth Farm was "a true farm, with pigs, chickens, cows, horses—everything a farm is supposed to have." Like William Ayres, Martin Knuth was progressive and raised a variety of items such as buckwheat, rye, and hay. Early on, he trucked vegetables to Newark and local markets, including the George Richards Company in Dover and the Wayside Inn in Denville.

The Knuths harvested and sold apples and peaches until the orchards were no longer productive. They operated a distillery in the carriage house, where beer, brandy, and wine were made on-site. A well and windmill provided the farm's original water source. Then, a German laborer employed during World War I (from 1917 to 1918), designed and installed a rife ram water system. A hydraulic pump in the stone springhouse (near Route 10) used the water flow of the adjoining stream to pump water to a 5,000-gallon storage cistern at the crest of the property. When needed, water flowed downhill to the farm buildings. The laborer's abrupt disappearance at the war's end sparked rumors that he was a German spy. Martin and Anna, however, were loyal Americans who became naturalized citizens by 1920. When Martin Knuth died in 1935, the prosperity his family enjoyed for 30 years soon followed. In August 1936, an intense fire claimed the barn. Here, Anna Knuth (right) stands with her sister in front of the tree that shielded her home from the burning embers of the barn fire.

The original 19th-century barn (like the c. 1890 barn above) was described as one of the largest in the state at 50 feet wide, 70 feet long, and three stories high. When lightning struck in August 1936, the timber framing caught fire immediately. Vehicles, livestock, large quantities of grains, and over 100 tons of hay were destroyed. Losses were estimated at $50,000. The barn alone was valued at $35,000.

Fireman fought the blaze all night and periodically throughout the following days, as the smoldering hay continued to catch fire. Anna Knuth mistakenly allowed a fire insurance policy to lapse after Martin's death. With no money to build a new barn, the existing c. 1885 icehouse and office (above) was moved and converted into a barn. Anna Knuth, with Susie, Frank, and Hattie still at home, attempted to start over.

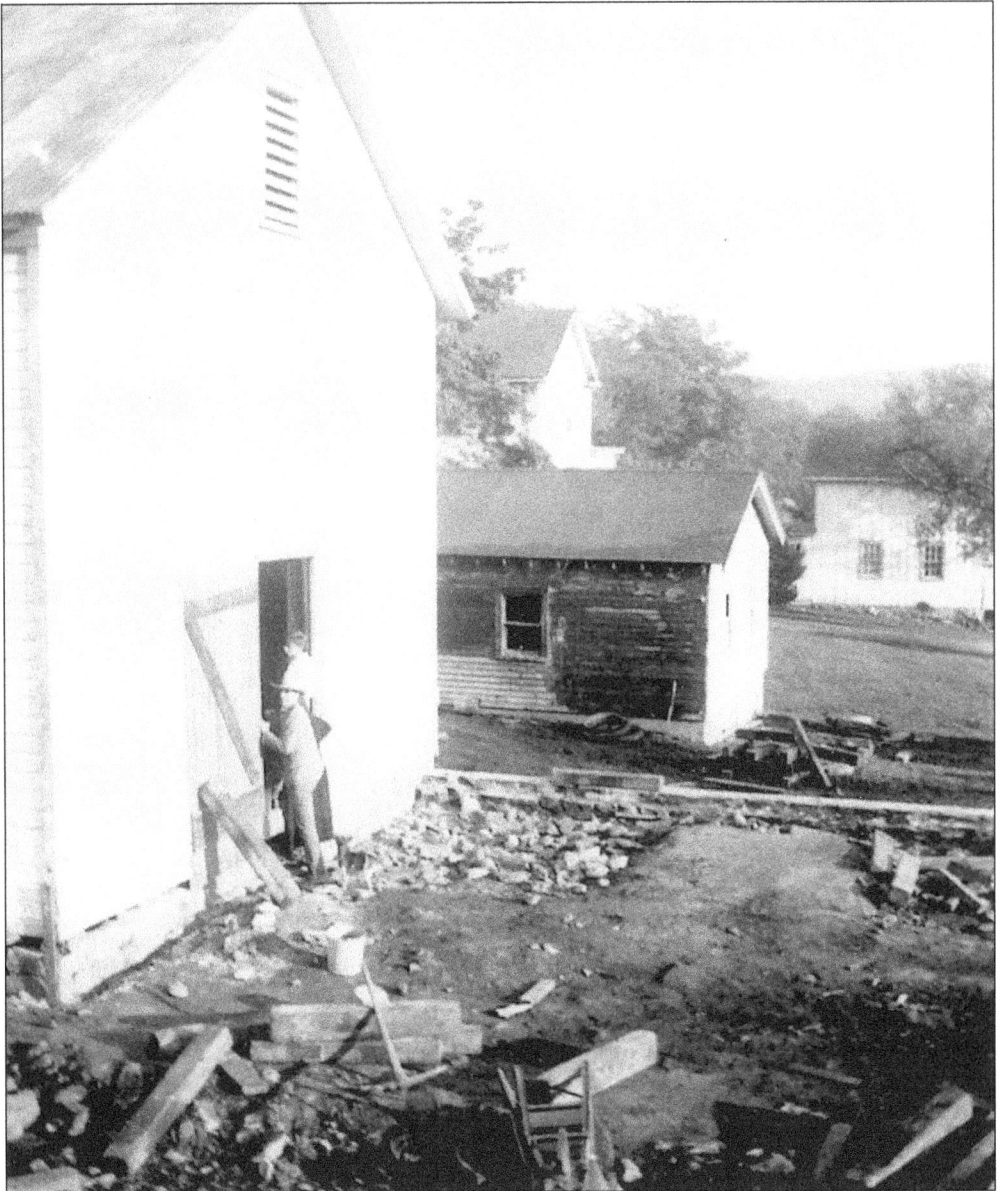

The transformation of the icehouse and office into the new barn c. 1936 is captured above. Stalls were fitted for livestock in back, with the front and second level modified for general storage and a haymow. The Knuths were never able to fully recover from the fire. Siblings Frank and Susie inherited the farm from their mother in 1950. Frank grew a variety of products including corn and hay, delivered produce to the local markets and grocery stores, and sold eggs to neighbors. Susie grew and canned vegetables and maintained an extensive flower garden. In 1985, Frank was unable to farm the property himself, so he leased the farming rights to local farmer Jeff O'Hara, who still farms there today. Despite many setbacks, Frank and Susie were able to remain on the farm until their deaths in 1990. They lived without many amenities or luxuries in the lower two floors of the farmhouse. Frank and Susie hoped that their farm would be preserved for future generations to enjoy. In 1996, Denville Township purchased much of the farm for recreational, historic, and open-space purposes.

Capt. Stephen Jackson of Rockaway often ventured behind enemy lines near Woodbridge, where his sister Anna Jackson Ayres (see page 37) lived with her family during much of the Revolution. Perhaps his warning of advancing British forces from nearby Elizabeth sparked the Ayreses' brief return to Rockaway in 1780. In Rockaway, they likely resided in Anna's childhood home—then owned by her brother—and may have been there during the visit of George Washington. Rockaway was Washington's headquarters for a few days in June 1780. Washington likely stayed at Stephen Jackson's home while he inspected nearby mining operations so vital to the American forces. Jackson was a member of Washington's bodyguard and his home would have provided a safe haven for both his sister's family and the distinguished visiting general. Three years earlier, tradition holds that Washington marched down Openaki Road through Ninkey on his way to winter quarters in Morristown, dispensing Hessian prisoners captured at Trenton with ironmasters in mines and forges along the way. This engraving was made c. 1844 by A. Daggett from the original painting by Colonel Trumbull.

Four

NINKEY

Sources suggest that Openaka was a chief of the local Rockawaka tribe of the native Lenapes, whose name became synonymous with the area around Lake Openaki. By the mid-18th century, this area was more commonly known as Ninkey. Like Franklin, Ninkey developed into a separate and distinct community centered on the forge that operated there along the Den Brook. Ninkey had its own schoolhouse, a tavern, a blacksmith shop, and two sawmills. There was also a gristmill that was used to grind grain for the Colonial army during Washington's second winter in Morristown, in 1779. The name Ninkey is said to have evolved from the creaking sound made by that gristmill's waterwheel as it turned. The turning waterwheel sounded like a voice saying, "Ninkey, ninkey." More likely, early settlers to the area perverted the Lenape name Openaki to Ninkey.

The Ninkey Forge was located on the west bank of the Den Brook on the dam. The area around the forge was originally part of a 500-acre tract purchased by John Losey (1700–1765) from Richard and Thomas Penn in 1757. John Losey was originally from Jamaica, Long Island. He moved his family to Morris County sometime between 1732 and 1740. Losey was already living in the area by March 1755, when Richard and Thomas Penn used his residence in Pigeon Hill as a point of reference in an advertisement for the sale of their father's lot No. 77. Some research concludes that Losey likely built the forge and gristmill after 1757, when he bought the forge site from the Penns. In 1780, the forge and gristmill were first documented on a map. It is also possible that Losey built the forge before 1755. Joseph F. Tuttle, however, claimed that Col. Jacob Ford built the Ninkey Forge prior to 1758. This claim is supported by J.P. Crayon, who wrote that Ford "built the forges at Shongum, Ninkey, and Franklin previous to [1750] as they were referred to [in 1750] as the 'Colonel's old forges' and located not far from Morristown his residence."

The historical record will likely remain in dispute as to who actually built the Ninkey Forge. James Puff Losey (1725–1778) came to own the forge after the death of his father, John Losey. At least one source claims that James built the forge. When James's wife, Mary Selee, died in 1784, the forge was sold at sheriff's sale to Joab Stafford, who also recovered 401 pounds and 4 shillings. The forge changed hands several times after that, before it went out of operation between 1806 and 1812. At least one sawmill above Ninkey was in operation by 1784.

A little farther north along Losey's Brook (later Den Brook) stood the Colerain Forge on land purchased by John Burwell from Thomas and Richard Penn in 1758. This site would later contain the first and second Union Schoolhouses (see chapter 5), as well as Clark's paper mill (see page 56). Unlike the forges at Franklin and Ninkey, no supporting community ever developed around Colerain Forge. Because of its proximity to the Ninkey Forge, it seemed appropriate to include Colerain in this chapter. The forge could have been built, or at least operated, by John Burwell. He was married to Catherine Losey (born in 1734), the daughter of John Losey and the sister of James Puff Losey, both of whom owned the Ninkey Forge. J.P. Crayon wrote that Obadiah Lum built "a forge at Coldrain before 1740." However, according to Joseph F. Tuttle, "It is possible that [Col. Jacob Ford] built the Colerain Forge also." Documents show that Jacob Ford held a mortgage at Colerain in 1770. Jim D'Angelo concluded, however, that "neither [the] dates of operation [of Colerain Forge] nor its owners and operators can be determined from the archival or historical record." D'Angelo speculated that since Ford was known to be heavily invested in the area ironworks, he likely financed Colerain Forge, while James Puff Losey (or perhaps his father) possibly built and operated it. Colerain is an American form of Coleraine, the name of a city in Northern Ireland that was Anglicized from the Irish Cúil Raithin, meaning "ferny corner" or "corner of the ferns." While it seems certain that Colerain Forge derived its name from the city of Coleraine, no one knows who gave it this name. Most likely, it was someone connected to the great migration from Coleraine to America in 1718.

Local historians have maintained that school was held at Ninkey shortly after the Revolution on the second floor of a tavern located on property now owned by the Price family near the old Losey house. The tavern-school was located on Openaki Road about two-thirds of the way from the corner and Mountainside Drive near Lake Openaki (or Openaka). Although some have attributed this tavern-school to "old records," it is more appropriately attributed to local oral tradition than to documented fact. The first written source of the tavern-school came from J.P. Crayon, who wrote in 1895 that "the present tenant house of J. Andrew Casterline was known as the half-way house for travelers, while the upper room was used as a school room, and probably ante-dates the Revolution." One historical account of the tavern-school remarks in jest that it "is hard to say where the spirits were most high—upstairs or down!" Some have called this tavern-school the first Union School, but it clearly was not. Rather, the tavern-school was the first of two schools at Ninkey.

In a letter to the editor of the *Rockaway Record* in the late 19th century, J.P. Crayon indicated that the tavern-school was still standing at that time but had been converted into a residence. He noted that the second floor of the old tavern not only served as a school but was also used for church services. He wrote, "If the school room could have remained intact with its original carvings on seats and desks, it would have been a curiosity for the people of today well worth visiting." Classes originally held in the tavern-school were later moved to a separate schoolhouse. The lone documentation of the existence of an actual Ninkey schoolhouse that was located near the forks in the road at Ninkey is a deed dating to 1813. Presumably, the schoolhouse was in existence prior to this date, although for how long is uncertain. It would not have been in use after the Franklin and Ninkey Union School was built in 1816.

John Stephenson owned this house in 1784 and lost it at sheriff's sale to Jacob Losey in 1790. The house was built between 1757 and 1784. At least three known documents indicate that the house was built by Stephenson. However, according to J.P. Crayon and Joseph Tuttle, Col. Jacob Ford (1704–1777) built the Ninkey Forge and this house before 1750 or 1758, and yet no documentation conclusively connecting Ford to the forge or the house has been found. Ford did have a financial interest in the nearby Colerain Forge as early as 1770. George Washington is said to have stopped at this house on his way to winter quarters in Morristown in 1777.

This c. 1895 view shows the Den Brook near the site of the Colerain Forge. Originally named for early Ninkey pioneer John Losey, the brook was once known as Losey's Brook. William Penn's 1715 survey refers to it simply as a branch of the Rockaway River. The first known documentation of the name Losey's Brook is found in the 1758 return from Richard and Thomas Penn to John Burwell. The same reference to Losey's Brook is also found on Col. Jacob Ford's 1770 mortgage on the Colerain Forge. In a 1787 Ninkey mortgage, the brook is referred to as Losey's sawmill brook.

The Ninkey gristmill and sawmill were at the same spot and operated with one waterwheel like the one seen here. A similar 30-horsepower wheel powered John S. Clark's paper mill (or Clark's and Brant's paper mill) between 1868 and 1875. The mill made pressed board (100 tons per year) using 2 tons of domestic rags, 111 tons of old paper, and 7 tons of cordage. The paper mill stood near the site of the old Colerain Forge.

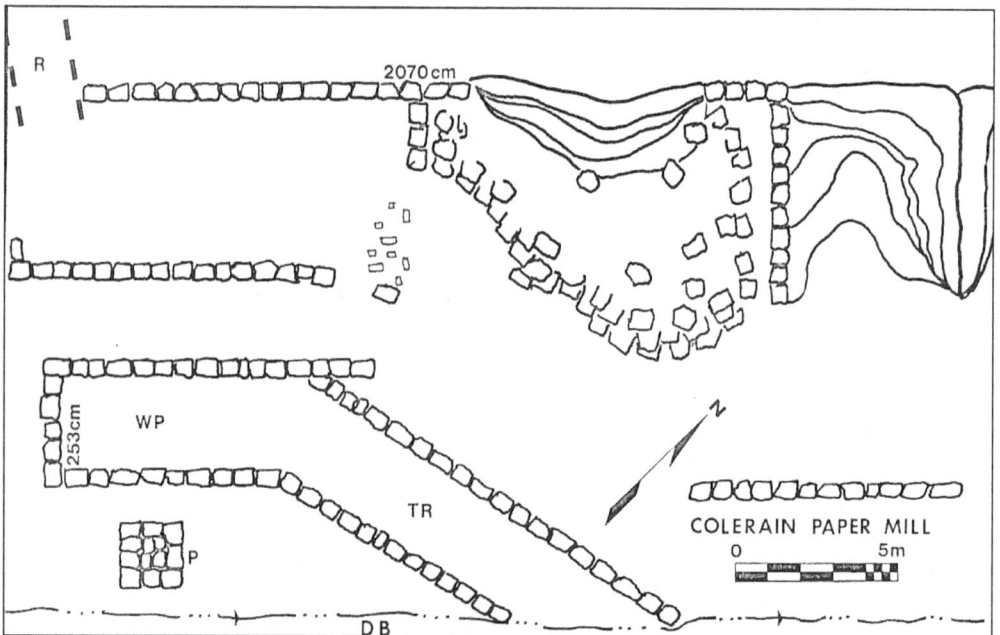

This diagram of Clark's paper mill shows where the water entered from the race (R), the wheel pit (WP), the wheel pedestal (P), the tailrace (TR), and the Den Brook (DB). Elam Brant purchased the site in 1865, built the raceway in 1866, and completed the dam by 1868. John Clark operated the mill until it burned c. 1875. The property was sold in 1876 to satisfy Elam Brant's mortgage.

The 1868 dam built for the paper mill created a small lake that came to be known as Laurel Lake for the abundance of laurel plants that adorned the shoreline. The lake became a popular swimming club by 1925. This image dates from *c.* 1930.

The Clark dam was intentionally destroyed by the state *c.* 1970 because so many area dams of similar age gave way during storms, causing considerable damage. Laurel Lake was no more, but the initials its members had carved on tree trunks along its shores can still be seen today.

Either John Clark or William Casterline built this house at 506 Openaki Road c. 1866. The house is shown here c. 1879 with some of its early inhabitants. Mahon M. Smith, born c. 1843, purchased the house from William Casterline in 1899. Mahlon was the son of John Smith and grandson of Garrett Smith. Mahlon Smith entered the Union navy in 1864, serving first on the receiving ship *Vermont* and later on the gunboat *Galatea*. After the Civil War, he went to the Colorado territory, where he worked in a sawmill on Boulder Creek. He bought land, built a house in Jamestown, and prospected for gold on Sugar Loaf Hill. When that proved unsuccessful, he camped near Long's Peak, where he hunted elk and other game and fished for trout. He then made his way to Cheyenne, crossed the Laramie Plains and the Black Hills, and landed in a place known as the Red Desert. He worked on the Union Pacific Railroad, which was under construction across the mountains. From there, he returned to Colorado for a while and engaged in farming before returning to New Jersey.

Back in New Jersey, Mahlon Smith married his cousin Emma L. Smith in 1873. He purchased the Clark house (shown *c.* 1900) and established a farm that was small but valuable, comprising 30 acres of rich, well-cultivated land. One account described Mahlon Smith as a "progressive, practical American farmer" who had "a good barn, substantial residences and outbuildings in abundance, and [was] surrounded with many comforts."

Mahlon Smith was a member and trustee of the Union school board, a trustee of Union Chapel, and assistant superintendent of the Union Sabbath School. His wife, Emma Smith, was the daughter of Isaac and Margaret Todd Smith, who taught Sunday school for 20 years. The Mahlon Smith farm along Openaki Road is shown here *c.* 1910. This was later the home of Leo Smith.

Some claim that George Washington stayed (or stopped) in the old house at 560 Openaki Road by the one-lane bridge traditionally associated with Col. Jacob Ford and John Stephenson and shown above c. 1895. While the story cannot be substantiated, it is conceivable that Washington could have been a visitor to this house.

At Ninkey, Washington is said to have had his horse shod by the blacksmith that occupied part of the old barn seen here, located on Openaki Road near Mountainside Drive. If the story of Washington's visit to Ninkey has any validity, it seems likely that his horse was shod here. With so many claims that Washington slept here and there, the less illustrious horseshoeing tale might just be true.

Seen are the one-lane bridge and dam at Lake Openaki. The dam is a large, cut-stone structure that extends around the entire northeastern end of the lake. The dam was built sometime after 1867, as the map on page 15 illustrates that in 1867, the location of the lake is designated as "the Bed of Old Pond." Openaki Road crosses over a bridge adjacent to the dam, at the dam's spillway.

This is the original home of early settler John Losey and later his son James Puff Losey. The house dates from 1755 and perhaps as early as 1735. John Losey and Jacob Ford have both been attributed with having built the Ninkey Forge and perhaps the Colerain Forge as well. While the historical record is unclear on this issue, they seem to be the most likely candidates.

In 1929, Wili (W.H.) Ebling (seen here) went to Nashville, where he was trained to prepare guide dogs for the blind. The Nashville climate was too warm, so Ebling offered the use of his home at Lake Openaki for the operation. Between 1929 and 1931, Lake Openaki was the headquarters of the Seeing Eye until it moved to Morristown. Ebling served 19 years as executive vice president of the Seeing Eye. This portrait was done by John Folinsbee.

The Eblings' Victorian-style home, shown here across Lake Openaki, was built c. 1885 as the lodge of the Openaki Association, a private hunting and fishing club. It was the first home of the Seeing Eye, from 1929 to 1931.

The current Openaki Bridge (shown here) was manufactured in Dover in 1900 and may be a one-of-a-kind remaining example of a one-lane truss bridge. The bridge abutments appear to be older than the bridge and older than that portion of the dam that is built against them.

In this c. 1900 view facing north from Openaki Road, the Union Chapel (center) and the Mahlon Smith house (right) are visible in the distance.

The Union Chapel is seen at its dedication on April 18, 1899. At the beginning of the 19th century, Presbyterian leaders called for greater religious education. Part of the purpose in establishing a new school at Union was to meet both the public and religious educational needs of the community. The early Union School was intricately connected with the evolving Presbyterian community at Union, separate from the main church at Rockaway. Sunday school classes were held there throughout the time the schoolhouse was in use. Prior to the building of the Union Hill Chapel that began in 1897, local Presbyterians held church services in the schoolhouse. The schoolhouse was often the focal point for church fundraising activities to pay for the construction of the Union Hill Chapel.

Five

UNION

In 1816, leaders of both the Franklin and Ninkey communities decided to establish one school for the education of the children from both areas. They chose a site by the four corners of Openaki Road and Mount Pleasant Turnpike, near the place where the Colerain Forge once stood. The "Franklin and Ninkey Union School" was built in 1816. It was a one-room stone schoolhouse located precisely midway between Franklin and Ninkey on the road connecting the two communities. The schoolhouse contained a coal- or wood-burning stove for heat. This was in fact the first Union School. There is one historical account of an earlier log schoolhouse within the limits of the Union School district that allegedly stood near the top of Zeek Road and was apparently still standing in 1895. The only information known about this school is that it was reportedly kept open only a short time in winter. Neither the 1868 Beers map nor the 1887 Robinson map shows a schoolhouse at this location.

The union of the two communities into one school district had a lasting effect on the area. The 1816 schoolhouse deed introduces the name Union for the first time into the Denville place-name lexicon. Eventually, the whole southern region of Denville became known as Union Hill. Old community names like Ninkey, Pigeon Hill, and Franklin, long associated with the area, gradually faded from maps and memories. Then, on May 16, 1860, after a failed attempt the year before, Union School district No. 6 in southern Rockaway Township (now Denville) and district No. 13 in Randolph Township were incorporated together as the joint Union district by trustees Charles J. Lamson, John A. Casterline, and Silas S. Palmer, with James H. Neighbour as superintendent for Randolph and Joseph F. Tuttle as superintendent for Rockaway. This later union of school districts in adjoining towns reinforced the growing reference to the region as Union Hill.

As best as can be determined, public school classes began at the old stone schoolhouse in 1816. Classes for the Union Sabbath School operated by the Presbyterian Church also commenced in 1816, although the church had been conducting Sunday school classes elsewhere since 1815. Records of the annual meetings between 1840 and 1860 provide insight into the operations of the first Union School. For example, they reveal that there were some repairs done on the schoolhouse in 1841 and that the formation of Rockaway Township was acknowledged in 1844. Also, it appears that personnel issues were a constant concern. In one instance, a teacher died just one month after the start of the school term in 1853. Most teachers, with few exceptions, remained in the school's employ for only a year or two. This means that searching for and interviewing prospective teachers was an ongoing task. Even with so much turnover, the records show surprisingly few incidents where a teacher was not hired for the school year.

In 1857, it was agreed that shade trees would be planted in front of the schoolhouse. Some of those trees still exist today. There was also discussion that year about building a new schoolhouse, but nothing ever came of it. The proponents of a new school were apparently not able to get the community behind the project at that time. At the annual meeting in 1859, an attempt to incorporate the school district failed. A special meeting was called later that year specifically to address the building of a new school. This time, a vote was taken and the notion carried, but only by a split vote (70 percent in favor and 30 percent against). It was then decided that it would be built near the road. However, the questions of whether it would be built of wood or stone and what its dimensions should be were left unresolved, and the new school was never built. Within the year, the community was forced to make those decisions as the quaint stone schoolhouse that stood for 44 years and helped unify southern Denville into one community came to a sudden and violent end. An arsonist burned the first Union School to the ground sometime between May 16 and June 18, 1860.

The teachers in the stone schoolhouse between 1816 and 1839 were Sylvanus Hance, Abijah Conger, Phebe Conger, Chauncey Hurd, Samuel Clay, John O. Hill, Mrs. Seargant of Morristown, Abby Gordon, Martha Crittenden, Joel Davis, Emily Hance, and Reuben Eaton from Connecticut. There were also teachers by the names of Hall, Roe, and Fisk. Teachers between 1839 and 1860 were Henry Axtell of Morristown, 1839–1842 and 1953 (he died this year); Mary Fordyce, 1842–1843; Catherine Rowland, 1843–1844; C.L. Dunham of Shongum, 1844–1845 (he was also a physician); C.M. Drake, 1845; E.D. Laurence, 1845–1846; Glover Gregory, 1846–1847; John O. Hill, 1847–1848 and 1855–1856; Charles Stickle, 1850; A.Z. Kitchel, 1850; James Cooper, 1850–1852 and 1854–1855; Edwin Tuttle, 1856–1857 and 1858–1860. Other teachers from 1847 to 1860 included Sarah Garrigus, William Peaslee, Miss Casey, Emma L. Wilson, and Mary Ford.

Members of the board of trustees, equivalent to today's board of education, were elected annually. Those serving as chairman of the trustees of the first Union School between 1840 and 1860 were William Brown, 1840–1843; Selee Tompkins, 1843–1844; Stephen Trowbridge, 1844–1845 and 1847–1849; Ezekiel Palmer, 1845–1846; Elias L. Palmer, 1846–1847, 1849–1853, 1854–1855, 1859 (special), and 1860; Simeon L. Casterline, 1853–1854; Miller Smith, 1855–1857 and 1859; David Y. Smith, 1857–1858; John A. Casterline, 1858–1859; and Joseph J. Ayres (special), 1860. Those who served as secretary of the trustees for the same time period were John O. Hill, 1840–1842, 1849–1853, and 1854–1860; John S. Follist, 1842–1848; Joseph J. Ayres, 1848–1849 and 1853–1854; Benjamin M. Wright, 1860; and John A. Briant (special), 1860. Those serving as trustees between 1840 and 1860 were Selee Tompkins, Elias L. Palmer, John A. Casterline, Silas B. Palmer, Stephen Trowbridge, John Smith, Alva Trowbridge, William S. Casterline, Joseph J. Ayres, William P. Casterline, John O. Hill, John W. Doty, John H. Lyon, Charles Lamson, and Silas S. Palmer.

The congregation of the Union Hill Presbyterian Church is shown c. 1963.

Some have claimed that after the union of adjoining school districts in southern Denville and neighboring Randolph in 1860, Pigeon Hill gradually became known as Union Hill. This, however, is only part of the story. The name's origins go back even further. Union Hill actually got its name from the union of the Franklin and Ninkey schools in 1816. The first Union School (1816) was destroyed by fire in 1860 and replaced the following year with this building (seen c. 1905), still standing at 502 Openaki Road. A school at Union would exist for 142 years.

Today, Girl and Boy Scout projects restore the covered porch of the second Union Schoolhouse and the outhouse, as well as provide a disabled access ramp. The historical society is supplying period desks and school artifacts, and trustee Art Harris is replicating the shutters.

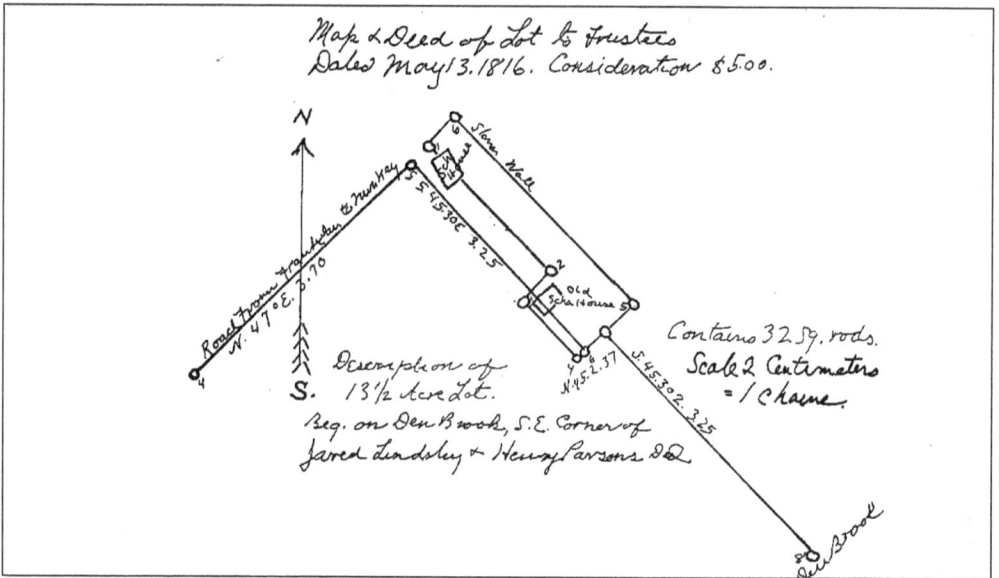

Map & Deed of Lot to Trustees
Dated May 13. 1816. Consideration $5.00.

Contains 32.59. rods.
Scale 2 Centimeters
= 1 Chaine.

Description of
13½ Acre Lot.

Beg. on Den Brook, S.E. Corner of
Jared Lindsley & Henry Parsons &c.

On May 13, 1816, Jared Lindsley, Ebenezer Lindsley, and Joseph Casterline sold what became known as the schoolhouse lot to Abijah Conger, Daniel Ayres, John P. Francisco, Samuel Palmer, Stephen Conger, and Jacob Vaness, the trustees of the Franklin and Ninkey Union School, for the consideration of $5. The above diagram is J.P. Crayon's plotting of the school property according to the 1816 deed description.

Joseph Casterline (1736–1832) purchased the corner of Mount Pleasant Turnpike and Franklin Road from Joseph Meeker on April 17, 1782, and built the original part of his home (above). Joseph's son William H. Casterline owned the house in June 1860, when the community convened there to post a $50 reward for the capture of the arsonist who burned the old schoolhouse and to finalize plans to rebuild the school.

The Union School was intricately connected to the Union Hill Presbyterian community that operated the Union Sabbath School there since the first schoolhouse was constructed in 1816. J.P. Crayon, seen here c. 1868, was associated with both the public school and the Sunday school and maintained detailed records for both. The magnitude of the community tragedy that befell the first Union School comes to light in Crayon's school records. On Monday afternoon, June 18, 1860, the taxpayers of both Rockaway and Randolph, residing within the newly formed joint Union district, met at the ruins of the old schoolhouse. At the very sight of the devastation, Joseph J. Ayres was elected president of the trustees, and Benjamin M. Wright was elected secretary. Afterward, by unanimous consent, the meeting adjourned to the home of William H. Casterline (see page 68). There, the trustees offered a $50 reward "for the conviction of the person who set on fire the old schoolhouse." Since the historical record makes no mention of the reward ever being paid, it is reasonable to conclude that the arsonist was never apprehended.

The meeting moved again to William Casterline's barn to accommodate the crowd. There, the taxpayers unanimously resolved "that we build a Schoolhouse this season." A building committee was elected, consisting of Silas S. Palmer, John A. Casterline, Charles J. Lamson, Selee Tompkins, and Benjamin M. Wright. Elias Palmer's building specifications were adopted. The new schoolhouse would be 22 feet wide and 34 feet long, with a center wall in the foundation running the length of the building, and with a chimney built from the foundation. It is very likely that the stones from the ruined schoolhouse were used for the foundation of the new building. The taxpayers agreed to take one year's school money and raise $300 through taxation and assessment to pay for the schoolhouse. It was decided that $216 be raised in Rockaway Township and $84 in Randolph Township to make up the $300. Construction was complete by 1861, when the trustees agreed to insure the new building against loss by fire. The second school was in use until 1908. Today, thick woods and old ruins can be found behind the second Union Schoolhouse. A century ago, however, sheep grazed along open slopes toward the Den Brook. This photograph was taken c. 1900.

Union School teachers from 1861 to 1892 were Job T. Dehart, 1862–1863; S.M. Stickle, 1863; William E. Magie, 1863–1864; John C. Bennet, 1864–1865; Quin Zeek, 1865–1866; Frank Berry, 1865–1866; C. Zeek, 1866–1867; T. Berry, 1866–1867; Mary L. Mills, 1867–1868; James Gillen, 1867–1868; Edwina Hathaway, 1867–1868; Austin Jones, 1868–1869; N. Kiser, 1869–1870; Kate Ayres, 1869–1870; William H. Hill, 1870–1871; Emma Cutter, 1871; Kate Ayres, 1871–1873, 1875–1878, 1880–1881, 1884–1887, 1888–1890, and 1891–1892; Jennie Owen, 1873–1874; L.J. Sawhill, 1874–1875; and E.M. Elmer, 1875–1876.

70

The second Union School is pictured c. 1900.

Seen here is the class of 1902–1903. Union School teachers from 1878 to 1895 were Neamiah H. Johnson, 1878; E.M. Bergen, 1878–1879; James Cooper, 1879–1880; William Most, 1881–1882; Lizzie C. Daly, 1882; Hattie E. Dutton, 1883; Eunice E. Tuttle, 1884; Alice Courtwright, 1888; Harriet M. Dalrymple, 1890–1891; E. Jeanette Foster, 1892; Susie L. Creveling, 1893; Lidie R. Youngs, 1893–1894; and Ellen Montjoy, 1894–1895. Kate Ayres (on the far right in the back row) and Margaret Dickerson (on the left in the back row) taught after 1895 and continued at the third Union School.

During recess, students often went down behind the school to the Den Brook. This photograph was taken c. 1895.

Chairmen of the Union School trustees from 1861 to 1895 were Selee Tompkins, 1861–1862; Joseph J. Ayres, 1862–1864 and 1879–1880; Miller Smith, 1865–1866; Aaron Hathaway, 1866–1868; John O. Hill, 1868–1870, 1882–1883, 1884–1885, 1887–1888, and 1889–1891; Simeon L. Casterline, 1870–1871 and 1876–1877; Jacob H. Fordyce, 1871–1872; J.A. Casterline, 1872–1873, 1883–1884, 1888–1889, and 1892–1895; Charles F. Smith, 1874–1875; Garret Smith, 1875–1876; Vincent B. Clark, 1877–1878; William S. Wright, 1878–1879; Elias L. Palmer, 1880–1881; John J. Smith, 1881–1882; and Daniel Ayres, 1885–1886. The secretaries were Andrew Casterline, 1861–1863, 1866–1868, and 1872–1873; William S. Wright, 1863–1865; William Ayres, 1865–1866; John O. Hill, 1870–1871 and 1881–1887; J.A. Casterline, 1868–1870, 1871–1872, and 1887–1888; William H. Casterline, 1874–1881; Franklin Hill, 1888–1889; Job T. Hill, 1889–1892; J.P. Crayon, 1892–1894; and William S. Eagles, 1894–1895. The trustees were Selee Tompkins, Silas S. Palmer, John A. Casterline, William Ayres, William H. Casterline, Jacob H. Fordyce, Miller Smith, Charles F. Smith, John O. Hill, John P. Hill, J. Andrew Casterline, Vincent Clark, C.D. Casterline, Frank Zeek; Stephen Ficter, S.F. Zeek, J.B. Palmer, John J. Smith, Job T. Hill, Daniel Ayres, Mahlon M. Smith, Franklin Hill, William S. Eagles, Peter Hopler, Isaac Lyon, J.P. Crayon, George Basley (or Bailey), and Louis Davenport.

In 1877, Denville's first library was the Union Sabbath School's circulating library. It contained 627 volumes of selected materials that were kept in a locked wooden pine box (seen here). The box was opened once a week to return borrowed books from the previous week and to permit readers to borrow new ones.

Opening exercises for the two-room third Union School were held in January 1908. Rev. S.H. Jones of the Grace Methodist Episcopal Church in Dover delivered the main address. J. Andrew Casterline (whose home is above and who was born in 1839) and C.W. Hall represented the board of education. Mary H. Rourke of the Women's Christian Temperance Union presented the school's first teacher, Margaret Dickerson, with a photograph of WCTU founder Frances Willard.

Church members believed that the 1816 schoolhouse deed contained language preserving the land's use for both public and church purposes since both had contributed to the building of the schoolhouse. When it was discovered that the deed contained no such provision for church use, the congregation, concerned that the schoolhouse could close its doors for religious purposes, began thinking about building a separate chapel.

The old bell from the original Rockaway Presbyterian Church is now kept at the Union Chapel.

Seen in June 1951 is the fourth-grade class at the third Union School. Teachers at the school were Miss Dickerson, Miss Smalley, Mr. Fisk, Miss Parker, Mr. Howell, Mr. Reeves, Mr. Muller, Miss Libby, Miss Harvey, Miss Philhower, Miss Boozer, Miss Guerin, Miss Trembirth, Mr. Juneiman, Mr. Bowlby, Mr. French, Mr. Davenport, Mrs. Cobb, Mrs. Hesseltine, Mrs. Pettit, Miss Underwood, Miss Hillman, Kate Ayres, Mrs. Blankman, Miss Mache, Mr. Steiner, Frances Downing, Agnes Downing, Mrs. Bruen, Mrs. Link, Mildred Lawrence Gill, Mrs. MacFall, Mrs. Smith, and Mrs. Brodeen.

This photograph was taken in 1957 at the groundbreaking ceremony for Lakeview School.

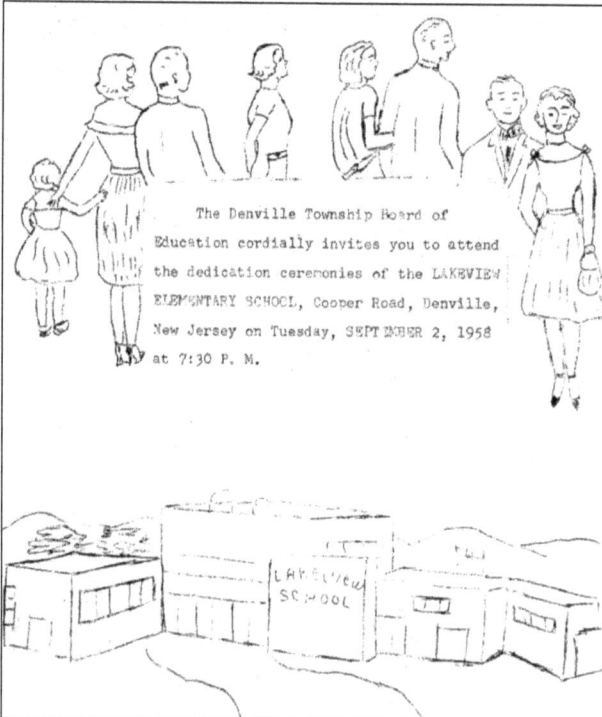

The Denville Township Board of Education cordially invites you to attend the dedication ceremonies of the LAKEVIEW ELEMENTARY SCHOOL, Cooper Road, Denville, New Jersey on Tuesday, SEPTEMBER 2, 1958 at 7:30 P. M.

Two teachers instructed all eight grades at the third Union School in 1940. Only kindergarten through the fourth grade remained by 1958, when the school closed and was converted to the board of education offices. Both the second and third Union Schools survive as reminders of Denville's early public education. The invitation to the opening of Lakeview School appeared in the September 1958 issue of the *Union Hill News*.

Lakeview School is seen in this 1963 photograph. The school opened in September 1958 with 12 classrooms and an all-purpose room. The school was designed for 300 students, but by 1963, it was accommodating 420 students from kindergarten through the fifth grade.

Seen is Mrs. Wincklhofer's 1963–1964 kindergarten class at Lakeview School. Seated on the floor are, from left to right, David Dickerson, Scott Cameron, and Allan Hull. Seated in chairs are, from left to right, Diane Harper, Bessie Ayers, Judy Fordyce, Linda Curtis, Diane Ackinson, Edith Witzler, and Donna Murphy. Standing are, from left to right, Mrs. Wincklhofer, Richard Weidman, Kenneth Summers, Glenn Johnson, Brian Quinn, Vito Bianco (the author), and Bobby Bell.

Winter arrives at the Cobb farm *c*. 1910.

Six

HILLTOP FARMS

The research of former historical society trustee Cynthia Hinson provides insight into the local farming scene from the early 19th century to the beginning of the 20th century. During the first half of the 19th century, agriculture in New Jersey experienced strong growth and resurgence. This was attributable to substantial advances in farming practices achieved through educational publications and agricultural societies and fairs and to the introduction of new farm equipment that was an outgrowth of the Industrial Revolution. As steel replaced the wooden plow, horses supplanted oxen as the power source, and fertilizers replenished sour soil, the state's agricultural output, which had been in decline, began to grow, and the number of small subsistence farms steadily decreased. At the middle of the 19th century, cattle and sheep continued to be raised profitably, and grains and grasses, which had established New Jersey's reputation as the breadbasket of the Colonies, were the primary crops.

In the decades following the Civil War, farming throughout the Northeast was heavily influenced by intense competition from the west, unprecedented and massive urban migration, and severe economic depression. The farmers who survived generally possessed better land and employed superior agricultural methods. Rapidly growing urban areas provided the key to survival for some, particularly for progressive farmers who actively sought new markets and willingly made changes in their farming practices.

Most farmers in the state customarily kept a few cows, producing milk for their own consumption and churning butter for sale locally. But as the market changed by the mid-19th century, many of Morris County's farmers turned to dairy farming as their primary form of husbandry. Technological advances and the growth of the railroad influenced the dairy industry, particularly with regard to the end product. During the 1850s, farm-churned butter was the primary dairy product, but by the end of the century, raw milk was more often sold to local creameries or sent by rail to urban markets.

Poultry, which played a small role in commercial farming earlier in the 19th century, started to gain stature throughout the agricultural community by the century's end. This was largely due to the efforts of the New Jersey Poultry Society, which was formed in 1877 in order to promote interest and encourage improvements in poultry farming and whose aims were accomplished by disseminating information and holding exhibitions. Toward the end of the 19th century, the growth of the poultry industry was boosted by the development of incubators and brooders. Increased demand from New York City encouraged the developing industry as well. The city, essentially a white-egg market, paid a premium for the light-colored eggs of Leghorns that were raised in New Jersey over the brown eggs from the western states.

In the early part of the 19th century, grains such as wheat, oats, corn, buckwheat, and rye had been the economic mainstay of the New Jersey farmer. With the passage of the Homestead Act in 1862, which opened western states with an almost limitless capacity to produce grains on virgin soil, eastern farmers found they could no longer compete. Wheat production, which in

New Jersey had increased due to improved soil fertility, reached its peak in 1870 and thereafter declined rapidly.

By the early 20th century, the state's agricultural scene was divided into three main areas: dairy farming, poultry farming, and truck and fruit farming. Many New Jersey farmers continued to practice a mixed husbandry. By not devoting all labor and resources to one venture, the average farmer of limited means could better avoid being without income for a portion of the year. While acres devoted to cultivation decreased, New Jersey farmers continued to grow grains, corn being the most popular. Sweet and white potatoes were also significant crops for New Jersey farmers, with tomatoes, string beans, asparagus, peppers, and cabbage being the most lucrative truck crops.

New Jersey agriculture during the early years of the 20th century was profoundly and adversely affected by increased urban growth. As cities and suburbs claimed a steadily larger percentage of the state's acreage, the number of farms began to decrease. In Morris County alone, the number of farms declined from a high of 2,554 in 1880 to only 1,128 in 1930. The total county-wide acreage devoted to farming dropped from 84 percent in 1860 to 32 percent in 1930. Technological advances, particularly the invention of the internal combustion engine, heavily influenced farming during the early 20th century. These changes included the introduction of the tractor, which replaced horses in the fields, and the truck, which supplanted the railroad for delivering produce to market. Electricity reached New Jersey households during this period, and by January 1935, over 51 percent of the state's farms had been supplied with power and lights.

Seen is the view from the top of Smith Road c. 1895.

Union Hill farmhouses were simple structures like the one above. Farmers recognized that their primary obligation was to the productivity of their land. This often meant that they invested any surplus income back into their farming operations and not into unnecessary luxuries of living.

Robinson's map of 1887 was the first detailed map of the area since the 1868 Beers map seen on page 31.

This *c.* 1905 image shows Garret Smith's old apple tree that stood on Smith Road, across the street from his house. The man standing on the tree limb illustrates just how old and massive the tree was.

History of Union Hill indicates that Peter Smith moved the right wing of this house "up the road" to this location. It also indicates that Robert Smith (whose relationship to the Smith family is not specified) attached the "little house" as a wing to his house (presumably moving it again). The main portion of the house above conforms to the remaining house still standing at 52 Smith Road.

This image likely shows one of the Smith farms along Smith Road, although just which one has not been determined. Perhaps it shows the "little house" after it was moved again to Robert Smith's house. A house on Smith Road belonging to a Mrs. R. Smith appears on both the Beers map and the Robinson map. Oddly, J.P. Crayon's research does not identify any R. Smith.

Writing on the back of the above photograph identifies this house as the Robert Smith house on Smith Road. This reference to Robert Smith, as well as the one mentioned in *History of Union Hill*, must be to the more recent Robert R. Smith, whose signature appears on the Union Hill Christmas greeting on page 2.

This is a closeup of the front steps of the alleged Robert Smith house on Smith Road, and the people shown in the photograph, while not identified, are presumably Smith family ancestors. If the account of the original Smith house (1750) in *History of Union Hill* is accurate, then the "little house" was removed from 52 Smith Road and attached to this house.

Leo Smith's home was located at 59 Smith Road *c.* 1900.

Here, the hay wagon is brought behind Mahlon Smith's house at 506 Openaki Road *c.* 1899.

Isaac "Ike" Lyon's house on Smith Road is seen in this *c.* 1895 photograph.

Ike Lyon tends to his animals on Smith Road *c.* 1895.

Nelson Cobb (1885–1982) poses at Ike Lyon's house c. 1900. Cobb's artistic ability led him to sketching and designing. He did some cartoon work for his own amusement.

Seen here is the bull pen on the Cobb farm c. 1895. Frank Cobb, Mary Ellen Ross Cobb, and their sons escaped the hot Newark summers in Union Hill boarding homes before moving here permanently in 1906.

George Smailes and his wife, longtime Union Hill residents, recalled that horses were kept at the Lawrence farm on Mount Pleasant Turnpike, also known as the Rock Etam farm. The farmhouse, now gone, was one of the older homes in Union Hill.

Here, 12 of the 14 children in the Miller family gather for a family picnic at the Millers' house on the corner of Zeek and Miller Roads.

Simple farm buildings, stone walls, and dirt roads were once commonplace in Union Hill.

Some 19th-century earthen dams and the ponds they created, such as the one seen here c. 1895, can still be found in Union Hill today.

J.P. Crayon sold this farm, seen here *c.* 1905, to the Cobb family *c.* 1906. Cobb family members still live there today.

Leonard Cobb (1886–1984) keeps his cow company while she grazes *c.* 1905.

The old barns on the Cobb farm are seen in this *c.* 1905 photograph.

Seen are the wagon house and storage barn on the Cobb farm *c.* 1905. The top floor is believed to have been used by J.P. Crayon as a darkroom.

Cedar Gate Farm, on Parks Road, dates from 1903. It was the home of Denville's first mayor, Frederick Eugene Parks (1913–1924).

Cedar Gate's large frame barn is one of the best-preserved barns in Denville.

The Cedar Gate barn is pictured *c.* 1969.

The original farmhouse at Cedar Gate Farm, located at 104 Parks Road, is seen *c.* 1910.

This is a later image of the Cedar Gate farmhouse. This is a two-story, Queen Anne–style home with a gable roof and now enclosed wraparound porch.

The old orchard along the hillside of Cedar Gate Farm is now a new residential development of single-family homes.

Parks Road is seen c. 1969, before it was widened. Frederick Eugene Parks built Parks Road so he could bring his produce to the Mount Tabor train station. He was a vocal supporter of Denville's separation from Rockaway Township and became the first mayor, in 1913.

Some young girls take a rest from the day's activities at the Union Hill Field Day in 1940 at Cobb's Field.

Seven

LEISURE TIME

Union Hill residents always made time for fun and festivities. The Spinning Visit was one of the customs of the 19th century. According to Sarah Ann Fichter, "one year one neighbor would raise a field of flax, another year someone else would do so." The flax bolls, or seeds, had to be removed. The stalks were then rotted under snow, and water softened and loosened the inner part from the coating. The flax fibers were then broken out and used to spin into linen thread to make clothing. In the springtime, the women of the area would come to the house on the farm where the flax was raised the previous season. They would spin the flax all afternoon and have a dance at night, when the local men joined them.

Sarah Ann recalled that dances in the area were often held at Cornelius Blanchard's house on Casterline Road. A house owned by a C. Blanchard appears on the 1853 Morris County map, in Hanover Township (now Parsippany), where Casterline Road and Old Dover Road meet. "This was a large house and it had a big garret that was not divided by partitions. Here the young people would gather and dance by candlelight to the inspiring music of the fiddler, probably some neighbor who excelled in this art. They danced the old fashioned dances and were very orderly about it. If anyone undertook to be rude or unmannerly to the girls, there were always plenty of brothers and friends at hand to see that the girls were treated with respect."

In 1842, 18-year-old William Ayres (chapter 3) began carting charcoal to Newark, New York, Brooklyn, and other cities to earn additional income. When he returned, his cart would be filled with hundreds of clams or several bushels of oysters, a portion of which he sold along the way; he shared the remainder with neighbors, who repaid the gesture on their subsequent trips east. Ayres's niece, Sarah Ann Fichter, recalled these springtime shellfish feasts as "clam classes and shad classes."

In more recent times, the Union Hill Field Day was an annual event sponsored by the Union Hill Civic Association between 1935 and 1941. It was held at Cobb's Field on the Cobb farm, later off Openaki Road, and was a day filled with fun activities, competitions, and good food.

Frank Cobb takes a leisurely stroll down to the banks of the Den Brook *c*. 1895.

The men get in a ball game on Cobb's Field during Union Hill Field Day in 1939.

Leonard Cobb takes a winter horse and carriage ride through Union Hill *c.* 1905. Leonard worked a short time in a Newark bank. That convinced him to become a farmer. He served on the Denville Board of Education in the 1920s and 1930s.

Frances Cobb (left), the wife of Leonard Cobb, and her sister Jessie Williams relax on the porch of the Cobb house *c.* 1906.

Local women take a leisurely stroll along the Delaware, Lackawanna & Western Railroad bridge over Franklin Avenue near Palmer Road *c*. 1905.

Frances Cobb (second from the left) and other local women rest in the shade *c*. 1905.

Nelson Cobb repairs the scarecrow *c.* 1905.

Leonard Cobb relaxes on an old-style country farm fence *c.* 1905.

A century ago, children on Smith Road enjoyed a good winter sleigh ride. This photograph was taken c. 1890.

Little had changed by 1960, when MaryAnn Bianco and the author rode their sled down their driveway on Palmer Road.

The C.D. Casterline house, on Casterline Road (later the Evans house), had a swing typical of the late 19th century in the front yard. This photograph was taken *c.* 1900.

Swing sets were still popular in 1962. Here, the Bianco children demonstrate the Palmer Road way to ride the swings.

Arthur Walther (left), Nora Crayon Walther (center), and Lillian May Davenport have a bite of lunch at Estling Lake on the way to the Hill Cemetery on May 21, 1916.

Seen here are the banks of Estling Lake near the Wright house off Franklin Road c. 1900.

Davenport family members rest on the Cooper Road bridge *c.* 1915.

Lillian May Davenport enjoys a quiet moment on the porch with her father, J.P. Crayon, perhaps in his last photograph, *c.* 1908.

Clark's Pond (pictured c. 1969), on Parks Road, was a public swimming hole and picnic area. There was a fee to park the car.

Fred Clark (Denville's mayor in 1968 and from 1970 to 1971) and the neighborhood children practice their ice hockey skills on Clark's Pond on Christmas Day 1961.

106

In this August 1960 photograph, MaryAnn Bianco (left), MaryAnn Cuneo, and the author cool off in the Biancos' backyard pool on Palmer Road.

Many a ball game has been played at Veterans Memorial Field on Zeek Road since it became Union Hill's version of Gardner Field in the 1980s.

The girls of Union Hill's 4-H Club compiled the above recipe book in 1952 from the women of the area. In 1948, they wrote a history of Union Hill.

Eight

COMMUNITY MINDED

Union Hill residents have always been active leaders of their community. Denville mayors Fred Parks (1913–1924) and Fred Clark (1968 and 1970–1971) have hailed from Union Hill. Other mayors include Calvin Lawrence (1925–1934) and Walter Luger (1976–1979), both of whom also served as Morris County freeholders. On the Denville Township council, several council presidents have also come from Union Hill, including William Barnish (1977), Daniel Craney (1980, 1981), Tom Gilson (1987, 1988), author Vito Bianco (1997, 1998), Pat Valva (2001, 2002), and the current president, Deborah Ann Smith. Other notable Union Hill residents include Frank Headley, longtime Morris County clerk; Ed Rochford, the current Morris County sheriff; Marilyn Cioffi, the former chairwoman of the Morris County Republican Committee; A. Richard Spinola, the former superintendent of the Denville schools; and Joan Murray, the current president of the board of education.

Union Hill has had its share of community groups and organizations as well. The Women's Christian Temperance Union (WCTU) is one of Union Hill's oldest organized groups. It was founded in 1902 with Mary H. Rourke as its first president. The WCTU played a central role in the dedication ceremony for the third Union School in 1908. The group fashioned itself after the National Women's Christian Temperance Union.

The Union Hill Civic Association was organized in January 1931 and has done much to help Union Hill take an active part in the life and growth of Denville and Morris County. Charles McCaffrey was the first president. The association sponsored the annual Union Hill Field Day. In July 1946, the civic association began publishing the *Union Hill News*, a monthly newsletter that quickly became a welcomed addition to the community. The *Union Hill News* served as a "community bulletin board" for Union Hill activities. Its "chatty, newsy style" kept residents informed of all that was going on. Occasionally, special editions contained photographs of community activities thanks to Samuel Gill, the printer on the staff. The *Union Hill News* staff also included Frank Headley, editor; Jennie Campbell, business editor; Vernon Joy, clerical editor; Leo Smith, sports editor; and Henry Pfannen, staff artist.

The Thursday Afternoon Club, a women's service group, began as a war aid society in 1941. Mrs. Charles Watts Sr. was the first president. The organization's initial project was to provide aid to the besieged English, who were then under Nazi attack. After America's entry into World War II, the group assisted the Red Cross. The organization's name was changed to the Thursday Afternoon Club after the war. The group's objective was to build a better community and provide entertainment and education for the women of Union Hill.

In June 1946, the need for an organization for Union Hill's children led to the formation of a boys 4-H club known as the Live Wires, initially headed by Everett Headley, and a girls 4-H club known as the Hi-Aimers, initially headed by Mildred Gill. There was also the Junior Hi-Aimers for younger girls, initially headed by Mrs. John Roggenkamp. In 1947, under the leadership of Hi-Aimers president Joan Garthe, Junior Hi-Aimers president Sandra Johnson, and Live Wires president Charles Helliwell, the clubs received first place for their exhibits at the Morris County Fair. In 1948, the Hi-Aimers wrote the first history of Union Hill.

The Union Hill Civic Association, the Thursday Afternoon Club, and the Union Chapel joined forces to establish a welfare committee, under the leadership of Emma B. Evans, to handle funds and provide for the needy families of Union Hill. After Evans's death in May 1947, the committee was renamed the Emma B. Evans Memorial Fund in her honor.

In April 1947, the mothers of children attending the Union Hill School organized the Union Hill School Mothers' Club. Its purpose was to promote better school-home relations and to assist in the program of education wherever possible. Many outside the community thought it strange that a mothers' club was formed and not a Parent-Teacher Association (PTA). However, it proved to be a wise plan. The fast growing community had much to do in the way of organizing itself before branching out into county and state affairs. After four years as a purely local club, the group became a PTA in June 1951.

Sarah Ann Fichter recalled that in the early days, "when there was a fire, every neighbor snatched up a pail, filled it with water at the spring and ran with it to the fire. There might be twenty pails of water carried to the fire. But the house generally burned down." The first Union Hill firehouse was built by the volunteer firemen in 1957 and would provide the community with a greater sense of security against fires.

The Thursday Afternoon Club is seen in this c. 1945 photograph. The group remained active from 1941 to c. 1960.

UNION HILL NEWS

UNION HILL CIVIC ASSOCIATION, DENVILLE, NEW JERSEY

MERRY CHRISTMAS TO ALL !

The first issue of the *Union Hill News* was published on July 1, 1946. Every month thereafter, it would advise Union Hill residents of upcoming events. Pictured is the front page of the *Union Hill News* from the December 1951 issue containing a Christmas greeting.

Jean Smith (left, center) and Eleanor Joy (below) participate in the balloon-blowing contest at Union Hill Field Day on Cobb's Field in 1939. Jean Smith was the winner.

Denville's Mayor Hughes (center) and other politicians join in the balloon-blowing contest at Union Hill Field Day in 1939.

Robert Thane (left), Hener Pfannon (center), and Chad Watts partake in a game of ring toss as two women watch at the 1939 Union Hill Field Day.

The men are off in the candle race at the Union Hill Field Day in 1939.

Eleanor Joy tries her hand at the ring toss at the Union Hill Field Day in 1939.

Here, the women line up for their turn at the candle race.

The Union Hill Civic Association sponsored the annual Union Hill Field Day, often held at Cobb's farm. From 1935 to 1941, this community-wide event was filled with fun, food, and festivities. This little girl enjoys dessert at the 1939 field day.

Grown men compete to see who could be the first to finish drinking a baby's bottle at the Union Hill Field Day in 1940.

Ruth Ayres (right) poses for a publicity
shot before joining the other dancers in
the Union Hill chorus line show in 1940.

The children of the first Union Hill co-op playschool in the late 1940s met at the Union Chapel or the Smith house, where the mothers took their turns at supervising the group.

More than 50 years later, Union Hill's concern for its children was still evident when the community pitched in to renovate the Den Brook playground on Mount Pleasant Turnpike.

Seen is the old Union Hill firehouse in 1963. In 1957, the Union Hill firehouse was built on the northwest corner of Route 10 and Franklin Road, on land leased from Scotty's Sunoco station for $1 per year. A 750-gallon pumper truck (unit No. 4) was transferred to Union Hill. Later, a 1960, 750-gallon-per-minute combination pumper (truck No. 6) was added. In 1963, renovations were made including a new meeting room and lavatories. Fire destroyed the Union Hill firehouse, an ambulance, truck No. 6, and all the furnishings in January 1965. Scotty's Sunoco provided temporary space. Fischer's Esso donated the current site for a new firehouse.

Mrs. Emmett Bupp presents Willard Ayres with an engraving from First Lady Mamie Eisenhower that was auctioned off at the Union Hill Fair Day c. 1955.

The Poulous farm (previously the Hopler farm), seen here c. 1964, dominated the landscape along Palmer Road since William Haden built the farmhouse in 1767.

The 1980s saw many farms disappear and many new developments take their place. The Poulous farm (dating from 1767) was lost to the Berkshire Hills development with more than 400 townhomes.

Nine

PROGRESS

When Frank and Susie Knuth died in 1990, the community became concerned that the farm they left behind would be lost to development like so many other Union Hill farms. Much had changed in Union Hill in the name of progress since Route 10 was built in the 1930s. The farms that once dotted the hillsides had given way to developments, condominium complexes, strip malls, and car dealerships. The committee to save the Knuth Farm (the Committee to Preserve Knuth Farm) was a citizens' group formally organized on November 21, 1991, with the ultimate goal of saving this one last farm. The original members of the committee and their respective functions were Howard Squire and Sue Schmidt, co-chairpersons and liaisons with the Knuth heirs, outside organizations, and advisors; Peter Maguire, public relations and communications; Frank Caprio, wetlands, threatened and endangered species, and migratory birds; Jeff O'Hara (the tenant farmer), farm quality; Vito Bianco, historic aspects; Mike Healey, government and development activity; and Debbie Denninger, fundraising. Several subcommittees were also established for various purposes that involved many more community volunteers.

The effort to save the farm would trigger sharp debate in Denville during the next several years over the advantages and disadvantages of open-space preservation. The farm preservation group ultimately realized their goal in 1996, when nearly 60 acres of the farm was purchased by Denville Township, but it would not be without compromise. A coalition of township-wide organizations supported the purchase of the farm but for different purposes than the "save the farm" committee. To recreational groups, more ball fields were tantamount to preservation. Furthermore, the location of the farm along a state highway meant additional tax dollars. The final compromise provided for two full-size soccer fields and a retail shopping mall along the highway section of the farm. However, a blueprint for future preservation projects had been established. Denville Township has acquired many hundreds of acres of land since Knuth Farm—some through outright purchase and others through similar compromises as the farm.

"The Shack," seen *c.* 1905, was the Cobb family's summer cottage, located off Franklin Avenue where the Prince of Peace Lutheran Church is today on Knoll Drive. The wood from the cottage was used to construct the porch at the Cobb house, seen below.

The Cobb house (formerly the Winds house) is shown *c.* 1905 with the addition of a new porch.

The gracious Cosman house, poised upon a 60-acre estate along Smith Road, was built in the early 1950s and is reminiscent of the style of the legendary Frank Lloyd Wright. The property was saved from development in a land swap between the contractor and Denville Township. Now, the development has been shifted away from existing quiet residential neighborhoods.

The John "Junior" Smith house is one of several historic homes along Smith Road that managed to survive. Others include Ike Lyon's house, Garret Smith's house, and Leo Smith's house, all more than a century old.

The Delaware, Lackawanna & Western Railroad was built through Union Hill between 1868 and 1887. The Dover tower on Palmer Road is shown above *c.* 1895. In the background is the Rockaway Road Bridge over the Rockaway River.

Seen is the inside of the Dover tower on Palmer Road *c.* 1895.

Large locomotives like the one seen here c. 1905 barreled their way through the once serene Union Hill countryside once the Delaware, Lackawanna & Western Railroad was constructed.

This photograph of Nelson Cobb fooling around was taken c. 1905.

A new water pipeline is installed on Palmer Road in the spring of 1933.

Orin Caskey and his sons saw lumber on Smith Road with modern machinery c. 1935. A few years earlier, they would be doing this by hand.

126

Leroy A. Davenport and his wife, Johanna, stroll with Lillian M. Davenport along the old wooden bridge over the Den Brook on Mount Pleasant (also Union) Turnpike *c*. 1915.

The one-lane wooden bridge used to be enough for the minimal automobile traffic that traveled the turnpike in the early 20th century. By 1947, however, an overweight truck was just too much for the simple bridge, and it collapsed. The one-lane bridge shown here replaced the old one.

Wright's railroad crossing (see page 33) was replaced with an underpass on Franklin Road.

In 1983, Union Hill was home to Denville's first heliport, located on Palmer Road.